Journeys to Glory

Journeys to Glory

PHOTOGRAPHS *Adam Bujak*

TEXT *Marjorie B. Young*

HARPER & ROW, PUBLISHERS

NEW YORK, HAGERSTOWN, SAN FRANCISCO, LONDON

JOURNEYS TO GLORY. Text copyright © 1976 by Marjorie B. Young. Photographs copyright © 1976 by Adam Bujak. All rights reserved. Printed in the United States of America. No part of this book may be used or reproduced in any manner whatsoever without written permission except in the case of brief quotations embodied in critical articles and reviews. For information address Harper & Row, Publishers, Inc., 10 East 53rd Street, New York, N.Y. 10022. Published simultaneously in Canada by Fitzhenry & Whiteside Limited, Toronto.

FIRST EDITION

Designed by Lydia Link

Library of Congress Cataloging in Publication Data

Bujak, Adam.
  Journeys to glory.
  Bibliography: p.
  1. Fasts and feasts—Poland. 2. Festivals—Poland.
3. Poland—Religious life and customs. I. Young,
Marjorie B. II. Title.
BR953.B84 1976   394.2'6828'09438   76–9953
ISBN 0–06–069732–6
ISBN 0–06–069733–4 pbk.

To our parents

Contents

". . . wherever religion comes to life it displays
a startling quality; it takes over. All else
while not silenced, becomes subdued and thrown
without contest into a supporting role."

HUSTON SMITH
The Religions of Man

Introduction

From antiquity, people have marked off certain days on the calendar and set aside work to come together with others—the family, the tribe, the village, the city, or the whole nation—to celebrate. After a period of festivities people return to their everyday routine, restored and refreshed. By celebrating, people keep in touch with their beliefs and with a specific community. Knowing that a particular occasion has been commemorated by parents and grandparents before them evokes the memory of their heritage—and of their humanity. As theologian Harvey Cox has noted, celebrating is a distinctly human activity, arising from "man's particular power to incorporate into his own life the joys of other people and the experiences of previous generations. Porpoises and chimpanzees may play. Only man celebrates."[1]

An unusually rich variety of religious festival can be found today in Poland, a country of more than thirty-three million people living in an area about two and one-half times the size of New York State. Before World War II, Poland was primarily an agricultural nation. Although still about half rural by population, it now is among the ten most industrialized countries in the world. A decade ago Poland observed its millennium, signifying more than one thousand years of Christian tradition. Many aspects of its contemporary culture are well known to the world. Jerzy Grotowski, head of Poland's avant-garde theater throughout the 1960's and early 1970's, is one of the leading dramatic creators of our time. Poland's Sławomir Mrożek now lives in Berlin; his plays have been produced many times in America. Polish composer Penderecki, and pianist Artur Rubinstein have been received with great admiration. The films of native-born Roman Polanski, now residing in the United States, have won world acclaim, as have those of Andrzej Wajda. Poland's colorful Mazowsze and Silesian dancers have graced stages around the world many times, including those of the United States.

In sharp contrast to these modern cultural expressions are Poland's diverse and numerous traditional rituals. With the possible exception of Italy and Romania, no other country in Europe honors so many religious holidays.[2] Among the most extraordinary of these festivals are a series of yearly celebrations which draw pilgrims from up to three hundred miles away. They come by train, bus, car, motorcycle, horse-drawn wagon, or on foot. Most come on foot at least part of the way, for some places are unreachable by bus or train.

In the smaller events, the pilgrims participate intensively for several hours and then embark on their journey home. However, some events involve up to a week of festivities. Pilgrims bring bread, cheese, and prayer books tied up in blankets slung over their backs. At the place of pilgrimage they form a temporary community with hundreds and, in some cases, thousands of others. Local villagers boil up kettles of soup and tea to feed the visitors and open up their cottages to house them. They spread straw on the floor and pack as many as thirty people in a room about fifteen by twenty feet. Those who do not find a place in a village cottage sleep in the church, in haylofts, or in fields.

The participants assemble to pray, sing, walk in procession, wade through rivers, and share stories, gossip, and food with fellow travelers. At the larger gatherings, a huge bazaar sells everything from cotton candy and frosted cookies to rubber balls and silver crosses.

Most pilgrims come to the larger events in groups called "companies," each led by a recognized moral leader in the home village. The pilgrimage begins and ends at the parish church; villagers gather there on the appointed day and return to be blessed when the celebration has ended.

Each observance centers around a particular religious holiday, including Epiphany which commemorates Jesus' baptism in the River Jordan, Lent, Easter week, and Mary's assumption into heaven.

Five of the eight ceremonies presented in this book are Roman Catholic, two are Eastern Orthodox, and one holiday is celebrated by the Marjawici Felicjanowcy, a small religious group which ordains women priests and bishops and sanctions marriages between priests and nuns.

Poland is about 95 percent Catholic; throughout her turbulent history Catholicism has been closely bound to her sense of national identity. When part of Poland was under Russian rule during the nineteenth century, at Christmastime Poles would burn a sheaf of hay and make a Catholic cross with the ashes in the snow to distinguish themselves from their czarist occupiers.

Seven of the religious festivals take place in remote rural areas, where people live by the rhythm of the sun rather than the clock and prefer to feel the ground under their feet rather than the city's concrete. Every Sunday the entire village streams forth to church in procession, and on Christmas they decorate small trees and place them on the graves of loved ones. This world contrasts sharply with the cities bustling with cars and shoppers; yet even in Polish metropolitan areas festivity plays a great role. On Christmas Eve people by the thousands jam buses and trams on their way to midnight mass. On Corpus Christi, a holiday celebrated eight weeks after Easter in honor of the Lord's Supper, they fill the streets with banners and song.

The rural celebrations reflect a world in which Jesus, Mary, and the saints are regarded not as distant, transcendental beings, but as intimate friends to whom peasants relate in everyday life. Since these people live off the land, one of their most frequent prayers is

for a good crop. Indeed, in many Polish peasant customs, pre-Christian agricultural rituals mingle freely with their Christian successors.

During each of the eight festivals believers abandon daily concerns and immerse themselves in another world, participating in a ritual which is meaningful to their lives. At every event fellowship is as significant as the particular ritual. It is the gathering of hundreds, or in some cases thousands, of people sharing a common belief which gives these events power. Hymn joins with hymn, prayer with prayer, story with story. The splendor and intense involvement in the several-day-long festivities calls to mind medieval European celebrations. Indeed, some of these events seem to be their distant descendants.

The larger pilgrimages also call to mind the massive rock concert at Woodstock, New York, in 1969. As at Woodstock, vast numbers of people of like spirit from many scattered places gather and live with one another for several days. Everyday human needs must be met, for example, food, water, sleeping quarters, and toilet facilities. Those who fall ill must be cared for. Meeting these needs is part of the fascinating story.

Unlike Woodstock, however, these happenings attract people of all ages. Young people break bread with mothers and fathers and listen to stories told by grandparents. At some festivals rock bands play self-composed religious songs, while other groups sing centuries-old hymns.

Perhaps the most significant difference from Woodstock is that people feel united, not only with one another, but with their ancestors. These celebrations are not the result of one year's spontaneity but are grounded in centuries of tradition. Most date back at least as far as the seventeenth century and have been observed every year since their founding. They take place in snow and in rain, in thunderstorms and in high winds, despite wars and despite foreign occupations. These events even survived the late eighteenth, the nineteenth, and the early twentieth century when for over one hundred years Poland was divided among three super powers and wiped off the map.[3] Today these traditions survive despite a system which says that religion is not necessary.

Although these pilgrimages attract as many as one hundred fifty thousand people, their existence is unknown to almost anyone except the participants. Even most Polish people do not know about them because each is limited to a certain region. Furthermore, the date, time, and place are not advertised on radio, television, or in newspapers: the tradition is passed from generation to generation by word of mouth. In most cases, a few weeks ahead of time the priests in the participating congregations post notices on the church door or announce to their parishioners when and where they are to meet to begin the journey.

Because these festivals are so little known, almost no foreign tourists or journalists attend. To the best of my knowledge, with one exception, these traditions have never before been described in book form. The one exception is the Marjawici Felicjanowcy, who are documented in several Polish publications and in a recently published book in English.[4]

That the outside world is aware of them at all is due to the efforts of Adam Bujak, an esteemed Polish photographer from Cracow, who began to discover these observances thirteen years ago. For fear of alienating his subjects and destroying their rituals, Bujak did not rush in with his camera. Instead he became a part of the phenomena, living and walking with his subjects, sleeping in their haylofts, and sharing supper with them in the evenings.

At first, people were mistrustful. Where was he from? Why was he there? But when he showed them that he had come, not to harm them or make fun of them, but to be one of them, they began to trust him and share their stories and experiences. Only after his presence had become accepted did he begin to take pictures.[5]

The trust he gained through participation allowed him to take unusually intimate photographs—so intimate that Bujak achieved a "subconscious identification" with his subjects. He says:

> My photography was born from a need to capture and preserve phenomena which I witnessed quite by accident, phenomena whose existence is unknown to the average twentieth-century person. When I came upon these relics of by-gone eras, I felt a need to inform others about them. I became convinced that what I had witnessed should not remain something between just me and these people, but that it should be added to our knowledge about contemporary man.
>
> . . . Photography as such is of secondary importance to me. What guides me above all is a desire to know life and the human psyche. The very fact of the existence of these rituals fascinates me, as does their psychic basis, which I try to penetrate.

So deeply does Bujak penetrate the "psychic basis" of his subjects that his photographs have been likened to the films of Ingmar Bergman.

When Bujak first learned of these pilgrimages, he was an amateur photographer. To earn a living he sold books, worked in a coal mine, and painted masks and scenery for a theater of the grotesque: he also delivered mail and carried caskets in funeral processions. When his colleagues heard that he was caught up in religious rituals, they made fun of him, saying, "We're here photographing beautiful girls, while you're off wading through the mud taking pictures of old women."

It was not long, however, before their laughter turned to awe, as they realized that he had uncovered a totally new and fascinating subject. Prizes gained for his earliest exhibit led to his becoming the youngest member—at the age of twenty-five—of the Association of Polish Photographic Artists, a prestigious organization of professional photographers, one of whose requirements for membership is to defend an exhibit of twenty pieces before a fifteen-person committee of art and photography specialists.

Ten thousand negatives later Bujak's exhibit of religious festival photographs has won acclaim, not only in Poland, but in Western Europe as well. Under the title of "Mysteries" it has been shown in the Musée Lorrain in Nancy, France, and Bujak has been invited to exhibit in Stockholm, Copenhagen, Paris, Athens, Rome, and West Germany. The National Museum in Wrocław, Poland, has bought the pictures for their archives. The International Museum of Photography at the George Eastman House in Rochester, New York, has purchased some of the photographs for their permanent collection. On the basis of this work Bujak was chosen by Swedish television as one of the five best photographers in the world for a documentary film on contemporary photography.

Wherever Bujak's exhibit has been presented, it has attracted long lines and provoked hours-long discussions. Many have asked Bujak from what film he took his subjects. They could not believe that the photographs were unposed, that such phenomena still exist today in the center of Europe. Many who have seen Bujak's photographs have requested a commentary on the subject.

The narrative which accompanies the photographs in this book originated in response to that request. It is based on my participation in two of these festivals and a visit to the site of a third and a fourth, which included conversations with local monks and some of the participants. It is also based on extensive personal interviews with Adam Bujak in Polish, during which his thirteen-year accumulation of facts, stories, newspaper articles, and documents hand-typed by priests was studied.

Our purpose is to share some beautiful and heretofore undiscovered phenomena with the rest of the world. The book was created to give people in our tragic and troubled times an experience of another world which is strange, thought-provoking, and inspiring. As Adam Bujak has stated, "Contemporary man, who has been shown rocket ships and other technical miracles, is in need of spiritual experience—experience which allows him to enter into other worlds."

Bujak is the only urban person in Poland who knows the location of all these events. He and I wish to share these festivals with the outside world, but in order to avoid their being overrun by well-meaning tourists, journalists, and scholars who might inadvertently contribute to their destruction, we have not divulged the exact names of most places.

In the course of time these phenomena may disappear or become commercialized. Already certain modernizations have begun to intrude. In some places cars are replacing horse-drawn wagons, and paved roads threaten to destroy the foot-worn processional paths. Some of the subjects of these photographs are no longer living. Hence, not only has most of this subject matter never been presented before in book form, but it may also soon die out.

Although we deal with religion, technical religious words such as *sin, redemption,* and *intention* purposely have been avoided, for this book is addressed to believer and unbeliever alike. It is for people of all walks of life. In it one finds an outstanding example of photography; some images call to mind contemporary films and paintings. Anthropologists will find a heretofore undiscovered aspect of Eastern European village culture. Theological scholars can observe authentic expressions of religious fervor. And in these festivals the avant-garde theater slogans, "Bring the audience in" and "Bring theater to the people," are fulfilled to an extraordinary degree.

Although these pilgrimages appear unusual, they speak to needs which are human and universal—forgiveness, fellowship with others, a sense of tradition, dealing with death and tragedy, offering thanks for what is given in life. They address the desire to look forward to something, to remember something with joy, and to stand in awe before the unexplainable in our universe.

The numerical order of the chapters follows the calendar year. Since the book has no beginning or end in the usual sense, the reader may begin with any chapter. The largest pilgrimage in Poland, that to Częstochowa where the icon of Mary attributed to St. Luke is kept, has purposely been omitted because it is well-known in Poland, has been written about before, and concerns an event specific to Polish history.[6]

The text and the photographs are intended to be experienced together, as a united whole. The reader should refer to the photographs whose numbers have been inserted in parentheses at appropriate places in the text.

Neither the photographs nor the text, nor the two taken together, present the whole story, for while this book opens up new and exciting subject matter, it does not exhaust it. There are many ways one could analyze the subject, but such analysis has purposely been avoided. Much has been left to the imagination and reflection of the reader.

The primary question which will no doubt cross the reader's mind is why people participate in these rituals. Some come to have a good time with old friends. Many come to carry out a tradition without which their lives would seem incomplete, just as our lives might seem incomplete without Christmas or Passover.

However, the deepest reason is also the most difficult to penetrate. What goes on inside the heart when one feels forgiven for misdeeds, touched by holy water, protected from harm, or that he or she has made a wish known to the Almighty is a mystery into which this book only begins to delve. Beneath the beauty of costume and liturgy, the awe at the sight of someone who resembles Christ, the thrill of thousands of voices joined together in song, and the joy of shared meals is an inward journey, a journey to something beyond oneself—a journey to glory.

Journeys to Glory

The Celebration of the Baptism of Jesus in the River Jordan

January 19 is carefully marked on all Eastern Orthodox church calendars. According to believers, on this day Jesus' divinity was made manifest when he was immersed in the River Jordan by the desert prophet, John the Baptist. Following the baptism, a dove from the heavens descended upon Jesus and a voice spoke, "This is my beloved Son, with whom I am well pleased."

Two thousand year later, adherents of the Eastern Orthodox faith celebrate this event by gathering at a river to watch the waters be blessed. Afterward, they carefully collect samples of the holy water to share with those who could not come and to keep on hand throughout the year. They will use this water to help fight illness in the family and, in the case of farmers, to ward off bad weather which may threaten crops.

The origins of this celebration may be linked to an ancient Egyptian festival which took place at this time of the year on the Nile River, supposedly at its purest during this period. Samples of the water were collected for special use throughout the year. Today water is still drawn from the Nile during the month of January to be used for baptisms.[7]

Our first journey takes us to a region in southern Poland, inhabited by Ukrainians of the Eastern Orthodox faith, as well as by Poles. We stop at a small village nestled in snow-covered mountains, with a river running through its center. Overlooking the river is a lovely wooden Eastern Orthodox church, surrounded by tall trees. As we walk toward the river, we hear a strange chopping noise. Coming closer, we see two men hacking at a huge block of river ice. From their efforts a six-foot cross emerges, sparkling in the bright sunlight as if it were made of silver. The men place the cross in a round hole cut into the ice and await the arrival of pilgrims.

But we do not stay here. The local priest has told us that not many people come to the River Jordan ritual at this place and that we would witness a more interesting ritual in the next parish.

After a few hours' walk, we arrive at a small town. A two-hour Eastern Orthodox mass is just ending as we approach the church. We hear old Ukrainian hymns and carols flowing forth from a crowd of almost two thousand. Since the tiny wooden church cannot accommodate everyone, many stand outside, participating in prayerful attention.

As the service ends, people move away from the church and proceed toward the river, singing and chanting. Banners portraying Mary, Jesus, and Saint Nicholas flap in the fierce winter winds (1, 2). Three men carry three-pronged candles which represent the Holy Trinity (3). As they trudge through the snow, the wind blows out the candles; they pause to relight them. Women pull up woolen scarves to shelter their faces, and children, resisting the temptation to throw snowballs, remain close by their parents.

After about one-half hour, the procession reaches the river. Still singing, the crowd gathers along the banks (4), and two men each place an undecorated Christmas tree in the water. Between the two trees they put a table, which will serve as an altar, and a cross about the size of a person, around which a white, hand-embroidered cloth is tied. On the

table they lay a liturgical book encased in a red velvet cover with gold metal trim (5), a bowl filled with holy water, and a small wooden cross hollowed out on one side.

The priest, dressed in white robes, turns to the men holding the ritual candles. He takes the candles one at a time and snuffs out their light in the river waters. Then he blesses the river by dipping his hand into the bowl of holy water and sprinkling drops into the icy stream. The people rush to the river's edge (6). They dip their bottles and cans into the river, filling them with the water made holy at this moment (7). The clanking of the bottles and cans blends with the eerie liturgical chanting and with the singing of hymns. Together with the whipping winds and the rushing waters, a strange music is created, punctuated by crow calls overhead.

Next the priest takes the hollowed-out wooden cross, dips it into the river, and, with swift jerks of his hand, sprinkles water on the people (8). The crowd sways toward him, and the singing swells as they try to catch at least one drop of holy water in their bottles. The priest closes the liturgical book and gathers a bowl of river water to be used at baptisms during the coming year. From the river's edge, he leads a procession back to the church, singing, "We wish you many years of life and happiness." When the people reach the church, they depart for home.

Many people follow the priest, but others linger by the river, still filling their bottles and touching holy water to their faces and eyes. Despite the winter cold, some wade into the river, scoop up water with their hands, and drink it. As one young girl splashes her face with water, she cries, "Oh, it's awfully cold." Her grandmother, gathering holy water nearby, smiles and says, "This is nothing. Why, I remember how before World War II people used to strip almost naked and jump into the water."

Most pilgrims who attend this ritual are Ukrainian farmers from surrounding villages and towns; an occasional visitor from the cities of Cracow or Katowice, where a Ukrainian minority live, can also be found. Most arrive and return by train. Just how long they have been coming to this place is not known.

Besides commemorating Jesus' baptism in the River Jordan, blessing the waters also symbolizes that the sanctifying action of the Holy Spirit is extended over all nature. The Orthodox believe that the Lord, by taking on human form, joined his life to the natural world. He walked this earth and was baptized in its waters. Hence, this celebration speaks not only to the human soul but to all creation.[8]

4

5

6

2

The Archbrotherhood of the Sufferings of the Lord

Our second journey takes us to a chapel in the medieval city of Cracow. It is the first Friday of Lent. In the chapel, we take our seats among a congregation of over two hundred people —men, women, and small children. Gathered in prayer, some kneel and clasp their hands before them; others sit quietly, their faces squinting and their eyes filled with tears. Still others lie on the altar and reach their arms out to the side, creating crosses with their bodies to remind themselves of Christ's suffering on the cross.

Suddenly, the black doors to a small room off the chapel open, and twelve figures dressed in black robes with black hoods over their heads emerge. Their leader carries a crucifix (9), and the two figures who follow him carry poles with human skulls on the ends. The next nine figures carry poles with metal-plate insignias on which are carved the sufferings of Christ (10).

These men are members of the Archbrotherhood of the Sufferings of the Lord, also known as the Archbrotherhood of Good Death. They cross through the chapel and into the main church, where they stand and wait for the ceremony to begin. Most people are so engaged in prayer they do not notice the quiet crossing.

As the period of private meditation ends, everyone takes a seat and sings the following song:

> The Lord, the creator of heaven,
> Hangs on the cross,
> You must cry for your sins, O people.
>
> O! O! He dies on the cross,
> Jesus closes his eyes.
>
> Most holy limbs and whole body,
> Cruelly beaten and hanging on the cross
> O! O! for you, O people,
> From his side the blood of Jesus flows.

The doors of the main church open, and the twelve brothers reemerge. The leading brother places the crucifix on the altar. The people kneel, and the priest recites the Way of the Cross—the fourteen major events in Jesus' last days from his condemnation at Pontius Pilate's palace to his crucifixion.

The recitation is echoed in fourteen paintings on the walls around the chapel, and several life-sized wooden statues of Christ recall his sufferings. One statue depicts Jesus praying in the Garden of Gethsemane. Loving believers have kissed its folded wooden hands so many times that the paint is worn off the fingertips.

The recitation of each station ends with the request, "Have mercy on us, Lord." Every now and then this prayer is punctuated by the brothers' chanting, "Remember, man, that you will die," sung first in Latin, then in Polish. Throughout the service, people come up to kiss the crucifix on the altar (11).

11

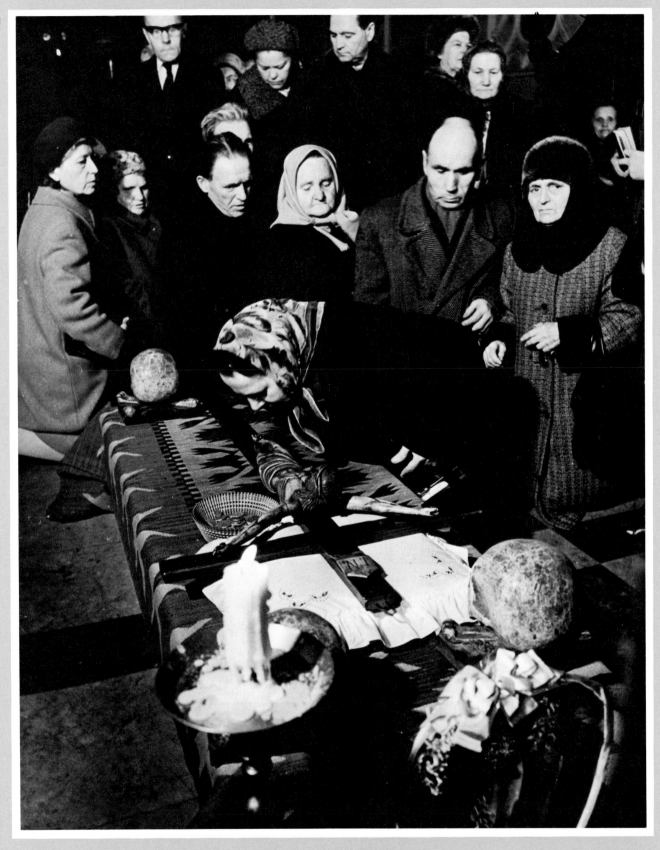

After the Way of the Cross is concluded, each brother lies with arms outstretched in a cross on the hard stone floor (12) while the priest leads the congregation in prayer for the forgiveness of sins. The brothers then rise to their knees and spread out their arms (13). The congregation joins them in this position, and the priest recites, "From bad air, hunger, fire, and war, spare us, Oh Lord."

In sharp contrast to the somber atmosphere of this ceremony, there suddenly appear little girls in Cracow folk costumes (14) carrying flowers in their hands. Four men in white surplices bear a golden canopy. At this moment the so-called Older Brother, the elected leader of the group, picks up the crucifix and leads a procession from the chapel into the main church. First come the other brothers; following them are the priest under the golden canopy, the little girls, and finally the congregation.

In the main church the brothers stand to one side while the priest leads the congregation in the liturgy, "Bitter Sorrows," which contains beautiful, poetic songs about the sufferings of Christ. This liturgy is followed by a mass, after which the Older Brother takes up the crucifix, and the other brothers their poles. Together they slowly proceed out of church and into a candle-lit, sixteenth-century vaulted corridor (15, 16). A choir of Franciscan monks joins in behind the black-robed brothers, singing the "Stabat Mater," a beautiful Latin song about the pains of a mother whose son was crucified.

> At the cross her station keeping,
> Stood the mournful mother weeping,
> Close to Jesus to the last.
>
> Through her heart his sorrow sharing,
> All his bitter anguish bearing,
> Now at length the sword had passed.[9]

The singing echoes throughout the corridor, punctuated by the ringing of bells.

Behind the choir, twelve teen-age girls carry banners on which is embroidered in gold threads the Mother of God, her heart pierced by a sword. Following these girls come the younger girls, who toss flowers on the altar as the procession reenters the main church, chanting:

> Holy, holy, holy
> Lord, God of Hosts.
> Full are the heavens,
> And your earth
> Hosanna in the highest
> Hosanna.

Returning to the main church, members of the congregation come to the altar to kiss the golden monstrance which the priest holds in his hand and which contains a relic, a tiny piece of wood believed to be a fragment of Jesus' cross. They sing, "We want God, Holy Virgin," and then gradually leave to go home. The brothers file out into the sacristy,

the room where sacred vestments are kept. They take off their robes and prepare to return to their daily routine.

In everyday life these brothers represent a wide variety of occupations—streetcleaner, photographer, student, painter, metal sculptor, comic-strip artist, porter (17), retired worker (18), carriage driver (19), and doctor of law and musicology (20). Once they don black hoods and robes, they become unrecognizable (10), reminding the congregation vividly that in death all men are equal.

This strange and beautiful ceremony is held every Friday at six P.M. during Lent, the forty-day period preceding Easter, which is a time for inner purification, penance for past errors, breaking sinful habits, reconciling with enemies, and almsgiving.[10] The main purpose is to make visible and concrete the pains and sorrows experienced by Christ during the last several hours before his crucifixion. The brothers also remind the people that they, too, will die, that death is an inescapable fate which meets all people.

This ceremony is the last remnant of a rich tradition dating back to the sixteenth century. The Archbrotherhood of the Sufferings of the Lord was founded in 1595 by the bishop of Cracow, Marcin Szyszkowski. At that time almost every church in Poland had some type of brotherhood modeled on the brotherhoods of Italy and Spain, whose influence in Poland was very strong. Their common goal was to pray for God's help to those in need.

Throughout its long history, members of archbrotherhood have represented a cross-section of occupations and have even included ruling kings and queens. Among its most prominent members were Jan Kazimierz, king of Poland from 1648 to 1668;[11] Anna from Austria, queen of Poland and Sweden, who entered the brotherhood in 1595; Andrzej Sborowski, prince and castellan of Cracow, who also entered in 1595; Maciek Bukowski, a professor of the Cracow Academy of Arts, who entered in 1617; Marcin Soczynski, president of the Appellate Court of Cracow, who entered in 1853; and Frederyka Wielkopolska, a countess who gave much money to the organization and also entered in 1853. Up until World War II, an elaborate initiation ceremony inducted one into the archbrotherhood, but this is no longer practiced.

At the time of its founding, the archbrotherhood maintained its own chapel and had its own priests. The brothers met weekly and held a service every Sunday. At one of their meetings the so-called Older Brother, who carries the crucifix or a skull on a pole and leads the group, was elected for life. Upon a member's death, the archbrotherhood conducted the funeral (21–24), characteristically chanting, "Remember, man, that you will die," as well as traditional funeral hymns. The brothers also took an active part in various pageants and religious ceremonies in the city of Cracow.

The Archbrotherhood of the Sufferings of the Lord not only performed ceremonies but also undertook humanitarian activities for which it became well known. The brothers regularly collected money and clothing and distributed them among poor citizens in

13

Cracow. They also visited the sick who lived alone and had no one to care for them, but perhaps their most astonishing enterprise was purchasing the freedom of prisoners and initiating them into the archbrotherhood. Annually, in consultation with the leaders of the main prison in Cracow and with the courts, the brothers selected one or more persons who were well behaved and truly sorry for their misdeeds. Sometimes they chose criminals who had been sentenced to death or to life imprisonment. They paid the prison a certain sum of money which had been collected from house to house and from the treasury of the city of Cracow.

On the fourth Sunday before Easter, those to be released participated in an elaborate ceremony, beginning with a mass in the so-called Lord's Room in Cracow's City Hall, located just above the prison. Following the mass, the names of those to be freed were read. Then there was a banquet, after which the freed persons walked in procession with the brothers through the streets to the cloister of the Franciscan fathers. There, in the Chapel of the Grieving Mother, the former prisoners prostrated themselves, beat themselves on their bare backs, and cried out for forgiveness for their crimes while the brothers and the families of the former prisoners prayed. At the end of the ceremony the exprisoners were given robes and thus became new members of the archbrotherhood.

The practice of buying people out of prison at Easter time flourished until the end of the seventeenth century when it was halted because of various corruptions. Nevertheless the archbrotherhood continued to grow, and in the nineteenth century it numbered well over a hundred members, most of whom were craftsmen. By the beginning of the twentieth century, membership had dwindled to about fifty. Shortly after World War I, the brotherhood also became known as the Archbrotherhood of Good Death, a name adopted from a similar organization which had ceased to exist.

During World War II, when Poland was occupied by the Nazis, the brothers still gathered to hold their services but dared not wear their hoods and robes. After the war the group was abolished as a social organization and became merely a group of twelve men who conduct a ritual every Friday during Lent. The Franciscan fathers took over ownership of the brothers' chapel and continued to collect money and clothing for the poor. Members of the archbrotherhood still assist the Franciscan fathers with the latter.

The archbrotherhood also has about fifty sisters, who participate in the Lenten rituals by holding lighted candles in the vaulted corridor of the church as the procession walks through that passageway (15). They do not wear robes or hoods, but inside their blouses each wears a medallion which portrays Christ on the cross on one side and on the other Mary with a sword plunged into her heart. When the sisterhood originated and what role it played in the early days of the archbrotherhood is not known. Some of today's sisters also belong to an organization of virgins who put on white dresses and white veils to participate in the Funeral and Triumph of the Mother of God celebration (see chapter 7).

14

Today the Franciscan fathers have expressed a desire to do away with the traditional costumes of the archbrotherhood. They say that although black hoods and human skulls were quite acceptable during the seventeenth century, today such practices are shocking and out of line with contemporary church procedures. The continued use of costumes is due largely to the efforts of Adam Bujak, who has been a member of the archbrotherhood for the past nine years. At one of their meetings he helped convince the Franciscan fathers not to interfere with this tradition.

As the brothers gather in the sacristy on Lenten Fridays to change into their ritual robes, they often tell stories from events in their daily lives. Perhaps the most unusual tales are related by the current Older Brother, brother Kabaj (25), who earns his living by transporting corpses to a dissecting room in a clinic. Kabaj frequently complains of an unhealed leg wound received during the Stalin era. A motorcycle ran him down while he was leading a pilgrimage to participate in the Sufferings of the Lord celebration (see chapter 3). Kabaj's conversation often displays a morbid sense of humor. One day when Adam Bujak entered the sacristy to change into his ritual robes, Kabaj exclaimed, "It's you, Adam, you're alive? Why, I thought I gathered your broken skull today. Look at my hands; they have wound marks from the edges of your broken skull. There was a photographer like you who fell down the shaft of a building and killed himself when he landed."

On another occasion, when one of the brother's skull got lost, Kabaj brought a substitute with him, which he had prepared at the dissecting room. Whereas the other skulls were gray and old, this one was bright white and had teeth which could be made to chop together. As Kabaj proudly showed the skull to the rest of the group, he said, "Look, just nine years ago this woman was alive; then her husband stabbed her and she ceased to exist. Now she's going to live among us in the archbrotherhood."

"Oh, enough of your morbid talk," replied another brother, "it's almost six o'clock —time to begin our ceremony . . ."

15

17

19

23

The Celebration of the Sufferings of the Lord

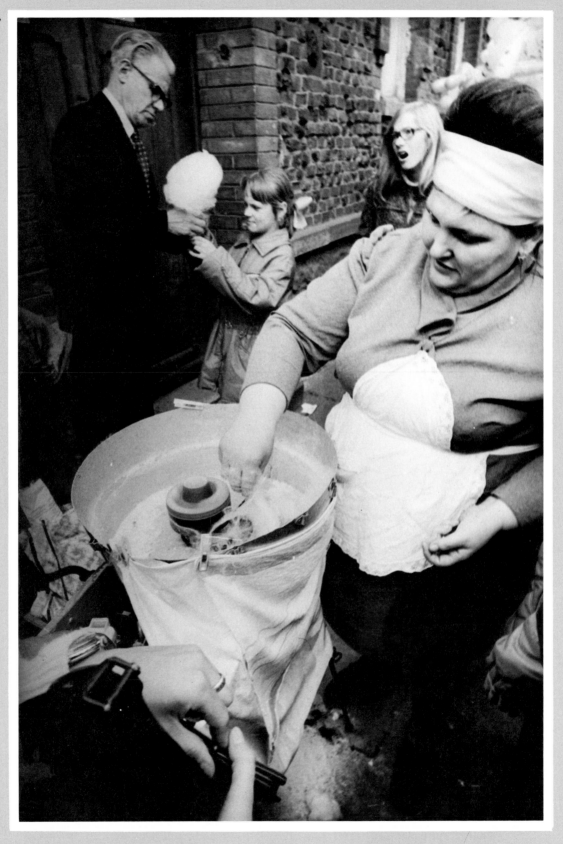

Our next journey takes us to a tiny town where we gather with fifty thousand other people to participate in the Celebration of the Sufferings of the Lord. Beginning with Jesus' entry into Jerusalem on donkey back and ending with his crucifixion on Golgotha, the major events of Holy Week are reenacted.[12] These incidents are not portrayed on a stage but take place in front of a series of twenty-four chapels spread out over a six-mile route in a terrain chosen in the seventeenth century for its resemblance to the Holy Land. Pilgrims come from miles around to live through Jesus' last days by walking with him from chapel to chapel, each representing an episode in his passion. These events are not condensed into a few hours' drama but unfold over a period of days which closely coincides with their historical timing.

On Palm Sunday a throng of about twelve thousand people gathers to accompany Jesus as he makes his entry through the gates of Jerusalem on the back of a donkey. The crowd includes young people in blue jeans, elderly peasant women in brightly colored kerchiefs, peasants, coal miners, and carpenters. All who have come for the first time wear wreaths of leaves and thorns in their hair.

As a white-robed Jesus and his twelve disciples emerge from an ordinary village cottage, the crowd cries out, "There goes Christ! There goes Christ!" Two monks from the monastery in this town lead a donkey toward him. Jesus mounts the animal, the two men leave, and two disciples take hold of the donkey's bridle. Together with the other disciples they make their way toward the gates of Jerusalem (26).

Opening a path for Jesus, the crowd throws palms and sings, "Hosanna in the highest, Hosanna!" The donkey, a bit frightened, begins to run. To match his pace, the pilgrims run lightly, too, and push forward, trying to get as close to Jesus as possible.

For nearly a mile, the crowd follows Jesus until they reach the cloister—the church and other buildings belonging to the local monastery. Just outside the main church, a group of ten merchants peddling sheep, medicines, fruits, vegetables, and caged doves have gathered on a raised platform. Some merchants are also changing money. Jesus approaches this marketplace and in a loud and angry voice cries out, "It is written, 'My house shall be called a house of prayer'; but you make it a den of robbers." He strikes the tables of goods with a rope while the crowd looks on intently. Doves fly up into the air, and goods fall to the floor. As the merchants leave, laughter ripples through the assembly. When all is quiet, a priest steps onto the platform and gives a sermon.[13]

The scenario pauses after Palm Sunday until Wednesday. During the interim more and more pilgrims arrive, making their way to the main church. Many have traveled several days on foot and are so moved by having at last arrived at this holy place that they fall down and make crosses with their bodies on the steps to the church.

After visiting the church, the travelers look for lodgings. Some spread their blankets in the fields. Others find places in the forests, in local haylofts, or on straw-covered cottage

28

floors. Still others set their belongings on a pew planning to keep all-night vigil in the church.

Most pilgrims come in companies, each bearing its own special cross or banner with a ribbon identifying the name of the village or parish. For the most part, people tend to stay with their companies throughout the week. During breaks in the reenactment they are led in song, prayer, and procession.

Between Palm Sunday and Wednesday, many companies walk the stations of Christ's suffering on their own, praying and singing. Often bands of trumpets, tubas, and flutes accompany them. As the pilgrims wind their way through the forests and hills, the singing and playing of the various companies blend together and echo for miles around.

From time to time the pilgrims take breaks to eat the food they have brought with them. To supplement their supplies, a bazaar outside the main church sells pickles, tomatoes, sausages, herring on bread, cotton candy (27) and large heart-shaped honey cookies with "I love you or "Be mine" or "Be true to me" written on them in frosting (28). Barrels of beer, orangeade, and Coca Cola are available to quench people's thirst. In addition to food, one can also buy hand-painted plaster statutes of Mary, of Jesus on the cross, of Jesus falling with the cross, of the heart of Mary, of angels, and of the saints. Also sold are secular statues—dogs, cats, elves, pairs of dancers, together with pocket mirrors which have pictures of Marilyn Monroe, Jayne Mansfield, and Gary Cooper on the back. Children can buy sheriff's badges, harmonicas, tin trumpets, and plastic guitars.

Most goods are privately made and are sold by merchants who come every year to all major religious festivals. Beggars also come and mill about in the crowds asking for alms, and Red Cross volunteers set up a station to care for anyone who becomes ill.

By Wednesday the crowd has swelled to about twenty thousand, all anxiously awaiting the next scenes in the Celebration of the Sufferings of the Lord. At 7:00 P.M. they regroup at the cloister, where Jesus' meeting with Mary Magdalene takes place. Playing the role of Mary Magdalene, a beautiful young peasant girl kneels before Jesus and asks forgiveness.

After a short scene between Jesus and Judas, a choir emerges from the main church and makes its way through the crowd, singing, "Jerusalem, O Holy Land." Dusk has fallen; torches light the way. When the singing has ended, a mass is held in the church, after which the people return to their sleeping quarters or remain in the church to pray.

On Thursday at 1:00 P.M. the drama resumes. By this time over thirty thousand people have gathered at the main church. Two Roman soldiers with trumpets announce the next scene, the washing of the twelve disciples' feet. Since this dramatic episode is enacted according to Roman Catholic liturgy, Jesus himself does not participate; he is replaced by a priest from the church. Dressed in white robes, the priest walks onto the raised platform where the disciples are seated. As each disciple removes his right shoe (29), the priest

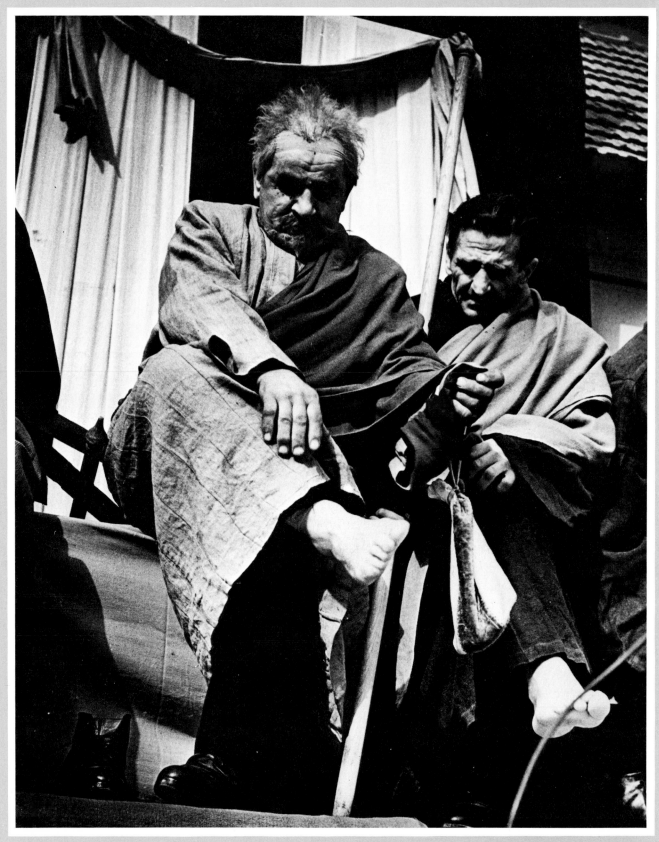

kneels before him, dips his towel in a white bowl of water, runs a light stroke across the foot, and leans over as if to kiss the foot. A choir sings as he performs this ritual.

The priest exits, and Jesus takes his place to celebrate the Last Supper. Turning to the twelve disciples, he says, "Truly, I say to you, one of you will betray me." One after another the disciples rise and respond, "Is it I, Lord?" When Judas also inquires, Jesus answers, "You have said so."

Jesus then takes a loaf of bread and breaks it in half. Holding the bread in his hands, he says, "Take, eat; this is my body." Then he breaks one half in pieces and distributes it to those on his left and breaks the other half for those on his right.

After the disciples have eaten, Jesus takes a golden cup of wine and turns to them, saying, "Drink of it, all of you; for this is my blood of the covenant, which is poured out for many for the forgiveness of sins." He passes the cup to the disciples, and they each sip from it. Silence reigns throughout this sacred moment, save for the singing of birds overhead and occasional coughs among the crowd.

After the Last Supper, Jesus turns to Peter and says, "Truly, I say to you, this very night, before the cock crows you will deny me three times" (30). Peter rises to his feet, draws his sword, and says, "I'll never deny you. Even if I must die, I'll never deny you."

At these words, the rest of the disciples rise and, with Jesus, leave the platform to take their place in a procession. Leading the entourage are three men holding a cross to which are attached the symbols of Jesus' sufferings (31)—the crown of thorns which will be placed on his head, the cross to which he will be nailed, the hammer and nails with which he will be nailed, the spear with which he will be pierced, and the sponge with which he will be offered vinegar. Behind these three men walk Jesus and the twelve disciples.

Thousands of pilgrims follow, singing mournfully, "He who suffered for us and was wounded—Jesus Christ, have mercy on us." When they reach the Chapel of the Garden of Gethsemane, Jesus separates himself and goes inside to pray alone. Onlookers crowd around the windows. As he lifts up his hands in prayer, his voice is heard through a microphone, saying, "My father, if it be possible, let this cup pass from me; nevertheless, not as I will, but as thou wilt . . ."

For several minutes Jesus prays silently in the chapel while the crowd waits. Then he rejoins his disciples, and the procession continues to the Chapel of Christ's Seizure. The chief priests and elders walk onto a raised platform in front of this chapel. One of the chief priests points to the crowd and says, "There's Judas, here he comes!" Leaving the crowd and approaching the chief priests and elders, a red-haired, red-bearded Judas asks, "Do you have the money?" They respond, "We have thirty pieces of silver for the blood of the Nazarene. But you must tell us which one he is." Judas replies, "You'll know him when I kiss him on the cheek."

Jesus and the other disciples walk onto the platform. Judas approaches Jesus, kisses

him, and says, "Welcome, Master." Immediately a group of Roman soldiers come onto the platform and push back the disciples. They seize Jesus and bind his hands with a rope (32). The crowd presses forward; some even push their way onto the platform and cry out, "No, don't take him!" While the soldiers hold back the protesting crowd with their spears, Judas runs away into the hills. The crowd laughs and jeers and then shifts attention back to the captured Jesus. Their sorrowful mood returns (33).

Jesus is led away by the soldiers (34, 35), the disciples disappear. Following Jesus, the crowd winds through forests and hills; some weep and others sing somber hymns. Already anticipating Jesus' fate, they sing,

> On the cross suffering,
> On the cross redemption,
> On the cross love of knowledge,
> O God, whoever can understand you even once,
> Neither seeks nor asks.

At one point they approach a river, across which stretches a small bridge. Since only a few can cross over it, the rest wade through the river, drinking freely from its waters, and dipping their hands in it and touching their eyes, ears, and lips. Some fill bottles with the water to take home with them.

After a few short scenes at chapels along the way,[14] the pilgrims arrive at the Chapel of the Council of High Priests and Elders (36) where Jesus' fate is to be deliberated. The high priest says, "I adjure you by the living God, tell us if you are the Christ, the Son of God." Jesus says simply, "You have said so," whereupon the high priest turns to the council and cries out, "He has uttered blasphemy. What is your judgment?" The council replies, "He deserves death."

Meanwhile Peter stands warming his hands by a fire below the platform on which the council is meeting. Dusk has fallen, and the fire glows, playing light and shadows across Peter's face. A young girl approaches him and says, "Do you know the man, Jesus of Nazareth, who says he is king of the Jews?" Peter answers, "Never—I never knew such a man; I never heard anything about such a man. I don't know him. I have nothing to do with all this." As he finishes these lines the cock crows. Peter repeats, "I don't know such a man, I don't know such a man."

At this moment Jesus descends from the platform and approaches Peter. Standing before Peter with his hands bound, Jesus looks into his face and says, "You don't know me, Peter?" Horrified, Peter falls on his face, weeping and crying out, "Lord, forgive me. I denied you. You told me I would." At these words, many in the crowd break down and weep.

According to certain of the Scriptures, after Peter's denial, Jesus was beaten by the Roman soldiers.[15] This reenactment does not dramatize the beating, and Jesus disappears

quietly. No further scenes take place on this day. However, those pilgrims who wish to experience this stage in Jesus' suffering descend into the basement of the Chapel of the Council of High Priests and Elders. They gather around a life-sized wooden statue of Jesus (37) whose hands are chained to a pole and on whose body wound marks can be seen. The statue portrays Jesus, not as an elegant figure, but as a simple peasant. Pilgrims place candles around him and talk to him as if to a friend. They stroke his face lovingly and tell him their problems. Some ask for cures or to be able to see or hear better. Others touch him with their rosaries, holy pictures, and prayer books. Still others kiss his hands and his face and prostrate themselves before him.

Many pilgrims spend the night in vigil around this statue or on the ground just outside the chapel. They build campfires to keep warm. Others return to the church to pass the night in prayer, dozing occasionally in the pews, in the confessional, or on the hard stone floor (38–43). Still others walk the path of the Sufferings of the Lord all night long. Those who choose to sleep return to their tents, haylofts, and cottages.

At six the next morning, the pilgrims assemble at this chapel. Jesus and the council of high priests and elders reemerge from inside. The council members say in chorus, "Let's take him to Pontius Pilate, for we are not allowed to punish by death." Roman soldiers lead Jesus away toward the Chapel of Pontius Pilate's Palace, while the crowd follows (44, 45).

There a servant steps out onto the balcony to announce the trial (46). Pilate enters, and Jesus is led onto the balcony by two Roman soldiers. Looking down from the balcony at the council gathered below, Pilate asks, "What am I to do with this man?" The council replies, "Crucify him, crucify him, to the cross with him." The crowd looks on in horror (47, 48).

Pilate answers, "I do not find any fault with this person. You take him and crucify him." The council members call back, "We're not allowed to punish by death. If you're a friend of Caesar's, then take him and crucify him." Once again, Pilate replies, "I don't see any fault in this man. Take him away and beat him."

Jesus is led into the chapel and sounds of beating are heard. When he comes out, blood is pouring from his face and hands. A red cloak has been placed around his shoulders, a sceptre in his hand, and on his head a crown of thorns.

Pilate speaks: "Go to Herod." The pilgrims move on to Herod's palace, but when they arrive, Herod looks out to the crowd and says, "I cannot do anything. Go back to Pilate. Maybe he'll help you."

Jesus and the crowd return to Pontius Pilate's palace. Once again the council members cry out, "Crucify him, crucify him." Finally Pilate says, "To the cross, to the cross." At these words sobs break out in the crowd. Two boys come out onto the balcony, bringing a bowl of water. Pilate dips his hands in the water and wrings them, saying, "I'm not guilty of the death of this man."

32

The soldiers lead Jesus down from the balcony and on to the next chapel, where a large, heavy cross has been prepared (49). As the cross is placed on Jesus' shoulders, weeping is heard among the crowd.

The crying increases at the Chapel of the First Fall with the Cross, where Christ collapses under the weight of the cross (50). The guards pull at his clothing and beat him with their ropes. An old woman from the crowd pushes forward, points to Jesus, and says, "Why do you beat this unhappy man? Enough of that—stop!" Another woman echoes her cries, "Yes, stop! Why do you mistreat him? He's done nothing wrong." At moments it seems that the crowd might actually lynch the Roman guards.

Rising to his feet, Jesus leads the procession toward the Chapel of the Heart of Mary, which is built in the shape of a heart. Here Jesus says his parting words to his mother. The crowd moves on toward the Chapel of Simon the Cyrene where Simon, standing among the crowd, is seized by two soldiers and forced to help Jesus carry the heavy cross (51). Together Simon and Jesus take up the cross and lead the procession to the Chapel of Veronica. A woman, Veronica, pushes through the crowd and runs toward Jesus. In an effort to block her from reaching him, the Roman guards hold up their spears. Despite their efforts, she goes up to Jesus and wipes his weary face with her handkerchief. Then she unfolds her handkerchief; the image of Jesus' face is imprinted on the cloth (52).

After this scene, Jesus and the crowd move along toward the Chapel of the Second Fall with the Cross. Here Jesus once again slumps to the ground; once again he is beaten by the soldiers, and once again he rises to lead the crowd on to the next chapel. There he meets the Weeping Daughters of Jerusalem (53) and says, "Weep not for me; weep for yourselves and for your children . . ."

Following this encounter, Jesus leads the crowd to the Chapel of the Third Fall with the Cross (54, 55). For a third time he sinks under the weight of the cross, now it seems, from real exhaustion (56). At this sight, the weeping crowd grows almost hysterical; their faces express great pain (57). People push through the guards and kiss Jesus' hands, his feet, his clothes. Some try to wipe the sweat from his body.

Inside the Chapel of the Third Fall with the Cross is a life-sized statue of a fallen Christ, surrounded by hundreds of lighted candles. Pilgrims enter and go around the statue on their knees, praying and weeping in an almost trancelike state. By this action they make a sacrifice to God of their whole bodies.

Outside the chapel, the three men carrying the cross with the symbols of the crucifixion (31) lean over and fall to the ground, as if to repeat Jesus' actions. Pilgrims rush forward and kiss that cross. Then begins the long climb up Golgotha, where Jesus is to be crucified. As in the Holy Land, the hill is steep and the path is strewn with rocks (58). As the crowd follows Jesus up the hill they sing,

33

People, O my people,
What have I done to you?
What harm did I do?
What grief have I caused?
I saved you from Pharaoh's power,
And you prepared a cross on my shoulders.

People, O my people,
I led you into the land of flowing honey,
You prepared for me a death with the mark of shame.

When Jesus reaches the top of the hill, he enters the Chapel of the Crucifixion.

The crucifixion is not enacted, but the sounds of the nailing onto the cross are amplified by microphone to the crowd, followed by these words: "You who would destroy the temple and build it in three days, save yourself! If you are the Son of God, come down from the cross . . ." Finally, Jesus cries out, "My God, my God, why hast thou forsaken me?" With these words the Celebration of the Sufferings of the Lord ends (59).[16]

Inside the Chapel of the Crucifixion, the bishop of Cracow says a mass which is broadcast to the throng outside. The pictures on the wall of the chapel are covered. No candles are lit; no music is played.

After the mass, the pilgrims regroup in companies and leave for their home villages to celebrate Easter with their families. They run en masse to the trains and buses or begin their journey on foot.

The departing pilgrims look tired from days of little or no sleep, of walking, of intensive prayer. One lady from a village about one hundred miles away brought with her a picture of Mary carrying the baby Jesus (60). She held that picture in front of her as she walked all the stations of Jesus' suffering. When she returns home, she will hang the picture in her cottage, feeling that it contains a special blessing. As she departs, peace and strength are reflected in her face.

Indeed a great strength can be seen in many faces as people leave for home. For several days they have forgotten their everyday concerns and immersed themselves in the experience of Jesus Christ's final hours before crucifixion. They have not been mere spectators but have actually participated by walking with him. Many feel as if they had been transported back two thousand years in time.

Perhaps this is a result of the costumes, props, and setting which are chosen with an eye toward authenticity. With the exception of the washing of the disciples' feet, which is performed in a liturgical manner, every event is carried out in realistic detail. A live donkey is used on Palm Sunday. Jesus carries a heavy wooden cross for several hours because two thousand years ago Christ carried such a cross for several hours. The climb up Golgotha is steep and rocky because it is so in the Holy Land.

As far as is practical, even the timing of the scenes approximates the biblical account

34

with one notable exception. The scenes on Maundy Thursday used to begin at six P.M. and end at midnight, as they are believed to have occurred originally, but because on one occasion in the mid-nineteenth century several people were trampled to death by the crowds in the dark of night, it was ordered that the scenes end by dusk.

Most pilgrims who come to this celebration feel a deep attachment to the place. Many have attended every year since childhood. The pilgrims comprise such a tightly enclosed group that they even have their own language, which is used in the scenes and in the conversation among the crowd. It is a dialect similar to Old Polish and is understood by nearly everyone who participates, even by those who come from widely scattered villages.

Despite the massive size of this festival, no central organization instructs people where to go or what to do. They simply know because their parents walked before them —and before their parents, their grandparents. If a child gets lost in the crowd, someone takes him or her by the hand to the next chapel where an announcment is made, and the parents come to claim the child. If someone is ill, pilgrims lead him or her to the Red Cross nuns on hand to give assistance.

General supervision for the preparation of this event is provided by the Bernardine monks,[17] who have resided here since the seventeenth century. The main director is Father Augustyn Chadam, who distributes the one hundred fifty costumed roles among the pilgrims and the local residents. Chadam has had no formal theatrical training, and no professional actors take part.

The roles of Jesus and the twelve disciples are usually played by pilgrimage leaders. They are chosen mainly on the basis of moral character although their physical resemblance to the personage is also considered. Once selected, they usually retain their roles for life.

Sometimes the players carry their roles into their daily lives. One peasant, when named to the part of Jesus, sold his farm and moved his entire family to this town. He played the role for twenty years. During that time he tried to live a good and humble life among the people, who often came to him for advice about personal problems.

Today a young man studying to be a monk at the Bernardine monastery plays the role of Jesus. The disciple Peter is played by a miner from Silesia. He, too, is sought out for advice in his village. A twenty-five-year-old farmer plays the role of John.

The person who plays Judas (29) cannot be a pilgrimage leader but is chosen from among the local inhabitants. He is a good man who plays the role simply because someone must play it.

The leaders of the pilgrim groups can usually read well, have a gift for oratory, and are recognized among the villagers for their high moral character. They must also have the approval of the village priest. Leaders do not raise themselves above the people; they speak to them as brothers and sisters, using the informal *you*. During the year they are sought out by the people in their village for advice.

36

Since the role of leader is usually maintained for life, as a leader approaches old age, he begins to prepare a younger person to replace him. He familiarizes this person with the special books that accompany the role, for they explain the meaning of each station of the Sufferings of the Lord Celebration.

The history of this awesome festival dates back to 1601 when Mikołaj Zebrzydowska, a wealthy Polish aristocrat, and his wife, Marianna, chose this town as the site for reconstructing Jerusalem on Polish soil. Experts were hired to stake out the site of Golgotha and the East and West Gates to Jerusalem and to lay out the twenty-four chapels. Great care was taken to make the architecture of the chapels and the distances between them closely parallel the corresponding buildings in Jerusalem. Hence some buildings, such as Pontius Pilate's palace, resemble secular buildings more than chapels.

The construction of the chapels took several years. The first Celebration of the Sufferings of the Lord is recorded to have taken place in 1609. Its development into a monumental theatrical event was primarily the work of the Bernardine monks who obtained permission from Zebrydowska to settle in this town and to use the passion story reenactment as a means to attract believers to the church.

As the festival grew, it attracted pilgrims from all over Poland and even from Bohemia and Hungary. A document from 1730 records a participation of twenty to thirty thousand. Because the monastery library burned down several times, further documentation of the first two centuries of the celebration is scarce and fragmentary. No texts from this early period have survived, making it difficult to establish possible links to medieval mystery plays.

The scenario currently used in the Celebration of the Sufferings of the Lord is based on Gospel texts, with a few apocryphal and traditional influences. To some extent the players improvise their lines from year to year.

With the exception of the period of World War II, this celebration has occurred every year since its founding. During the nineteenth century when Poland was divided among the German, Austro-Hungarian, and Russian Empires, great care was taken to distribute the roles of the twelve disciples among representatives of each of the three Polish sectors.

In recent years more and more intellectuals from the cities have been drawn to this event, including the famous film director, Andrzej Wajda. Those with an interest in avant-garde theater are especially attracted, for here they find a drama in which there is virtually no barrier between actor and spectator, an experience which truly engages the audience. One reason for this deep involvement is the realism with which the events are reenacted; the other and perhaps more fundamental reason is that the pilgrims bring to this experience a deep faith rooted in centuries of tradition.

38

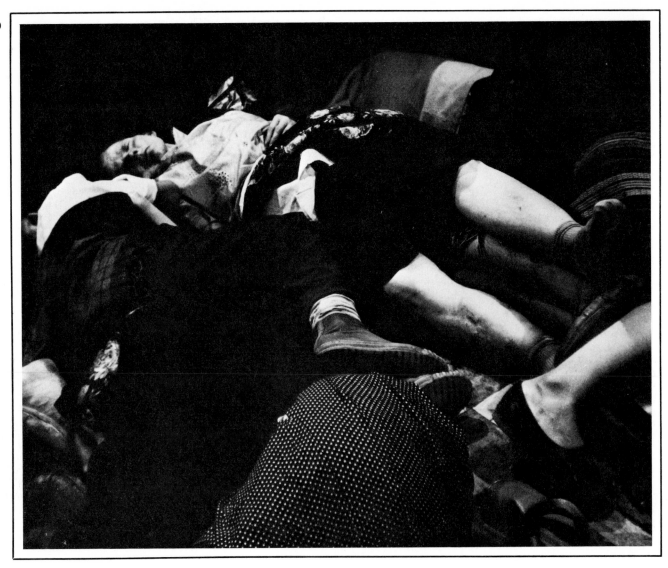

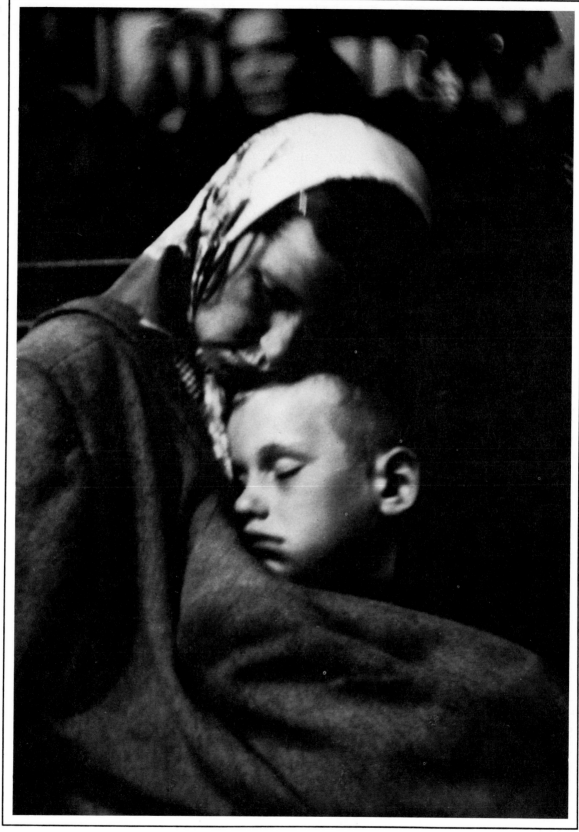

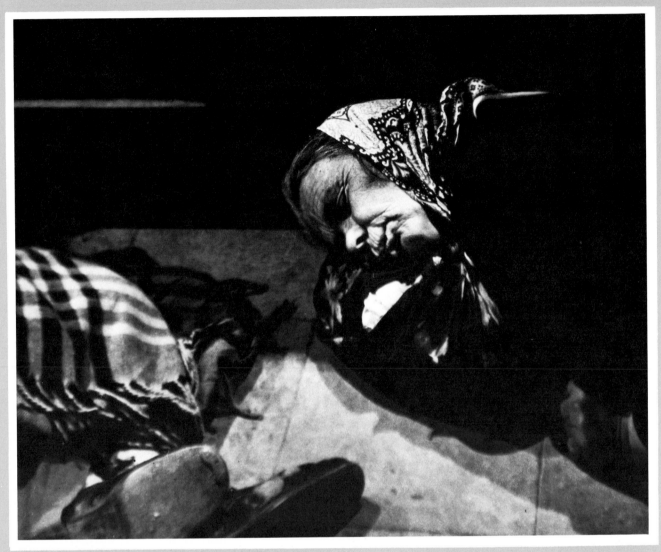

47

54

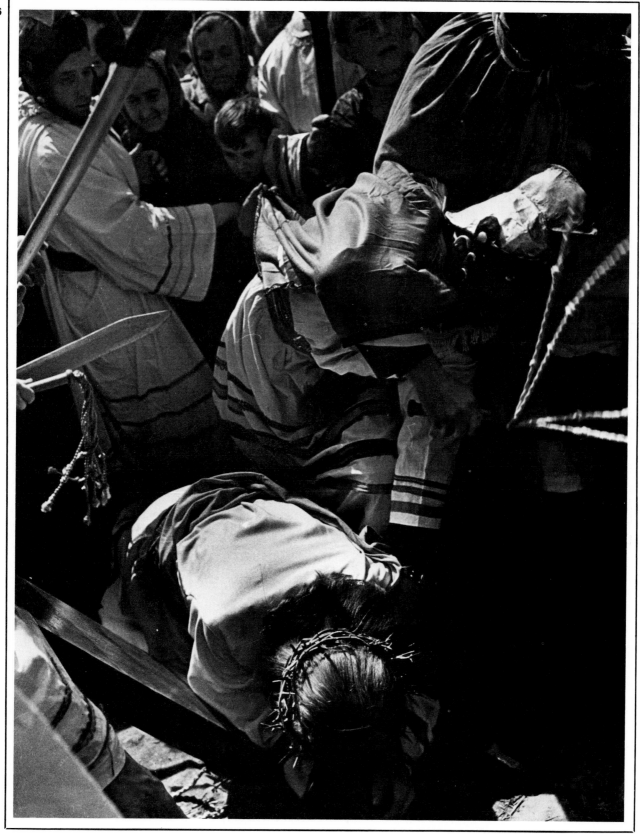

59

The Procession on One Hundred Horses

63

Throughout Poland Easter is celebrated with much festivity and elaborate preparation. It is a season perhaps even more joyous than Christmas. The village cottage is thoroughly swept; walls and ceilings are whitewashed; and the wooden furniture is scrubbed and polished. The main room is decorated with potted plants and delicately cut-out paper flowers. The courtyard, stables, and barns are put in order. In the evenings girls gather in one another's homes to make "pisanki"—intricately patterned colored eggs—a tradition which dates back to the eleventh century.[18] Special mound cakes with twigs of green stuck in the center are prepared. White lambs made of sugar, wood, or cake with white frosting are sold in the stores. Each lamb represents the risen Christ and carries a red banner with a white cross in the center.

On Holy Saturday, samples of every food to be eaten at the special Easter Eve meal are taken to the church in baskets to be blessed—breads, hams, sausages, cheese, fruits, salt, eggs, and cakes. Also on this day, people visit the grave of Christ in the church. This grave is usually above ground, and on it lies a life-sized wooden statue of Christ. On this day the grave is surrounded by hundreds of flowers. The holy pictures in the church are covered with purple cloths, and the ciborium containing the holy sacrament is opened. The wafer, representing the body of Christ, is placed on a wooden plank jutting out above Christ's grave.

At dawn on Easter Sunday young and old alike stream forth in procession to celebrate the 6:00 A.M. resurrection mass, the holiest service of the year. After church, families exchange visits and gather around the table to eat the newly blessed foods.

In Poland Easter does not end on Sunday but continues on Monday, *Smigus Dyngus.* On this day people drench one another with water to evoke the rains needed for spring sowing. A pretty girl is especially vulnerable to this capricious tradition. Boys may even wait on the roof of her home, ready to dump a bucket of water on her the minute she appears.

Other Easter Monday festivities vary from region to region. In some areas there is a street fair where hand-carved wooden statues, cut-out paper flowers, sugar lambs, and foods of all kinds are sold. In other areas there is dancing in folk costumes to the tunes of energetic bands. And on this day a tidily kept little village in the southwest corner of Poland observes an unusual tradition called the Procession on One Hundred Horses. In this region Polish, Moravian, and German cultural influences converge and can be observed in the architecture, clothing, and everyday language.

We gather for this festivity at the square in front of the Roman Catholic church at 12:30 on Easter Monday. As the church bells ring out, roughly one hundred horses and riders line up at the square. Each horse has a specially designated place. These are ordinary work horses, but of remarkable beauty. Days in advance they are cleaned, their coats are polished, and their hooves are painted with black laquer. Their saddles and bridles are

graced with jewellike metal decorations. As the horses and riders stand in line waiting for the march to begin, they call to mind a military brigade or a company of knights.

For a second time the church bells ring out. This is the signal for the priest, dressed in long golden robes, to come out from his home and climb on a horse which has been specially prepared for him (61). With his two assistants he rides toward the line-up of horses and takes his place. A twenty-piece band, also on horseback, strikes up a tune, and the cavalcade moves forward.

As the riders trot along, they sing Moravian and Polish Easter hymns and songs of prayer for a successful harvest accompanied by the church bells and the clicking of horse hooves on the asphalt path (62).

The first horseman carries a cross, flanked on either side by a horseman carrying a banner. Behind the first line one rider carries a wooden statue of a risen Christ (63), and another carries a statue of Christ on the cross. Next comes the priest, and after him, the town band composed of trumpets, tubas, saxophones, and drums, each played by a villager (64). The rest of the riders follow the band. About four thousand people take part in this event, but only men participate on horseback; women, children, and other pilgrims follow on foot (65) or in automobiles. Those who come in pilgrimage are mostly relatives from nearby villages.

The first goal, about four miles away, is a tiny wooden church built in the seventeenth century and known as the Church of the Holy Cross. It is surrounded by neat little paths, and nearby is a park with well-mowed grass and clean benches. Encircling the church are fields of rye, corn, and potatoes.

At the church the horsemen dismount, tie their horses to trees and fenceposts, and enter to participate in a ritual which includes special blessings for the year's crop. The service is amplified through microphones to the onlookers sitting on benches in the park outside.

At the end of the service the riders emerge from the church. As two trumpeters announce the next lap of the procession, the riders mount their horses and canter across the fields, singing prayerful songs for a successful harvest. No one accompanies the procession during this leg of the journey. As we retrace our steps along the asphalt path to the village, the horses disappear from view (66), and the singing of the riders and the playing of the band gradually fade away in the distance.

At about 4:30 we line up at the edge of the village to welcome home the horses and riders. For the last eight hundred yards of the journey, they race (67, 68). Everyone takes part except the priest and the band. As the horses gallop down the path, we hear enthusiastic cries: "Here they come! Here they come! Our Wojtek is first!" No prizes are given, but it is a great honor to win.

At the end of the race, the horsemen once again form a procession and silently ride toward the church where they dismount. The whole village joins them for a service.

65

Although the precise origins of the Procession on One Hundred Horses are unknown, this celebration is believed to have begun some three hundred years ago. Similar festivities on Easter Monday also take place in Bavaria, in Słowian Łużyckich in East Germany, and in a few other parishes in the diocese of Poland.

The Procession on One Hundred Horses is organized by the local priest, who holds great authority in the village. People come to him not only with personal problems, but with problems of agriculture as well. He works closely with the organization that helps run the village's farms. From this association individual farmers can rent heavy machinery, including tractors, plows, and combines.

The horses participating in the Procession on One Hundred Horses are used only for light work, such as hauling pigs and sheep to market. As the village employs more and more machinery, the horses are becoming almost a hobby; yet the tradition of the Procession on One Hundred Horses is so deeply imbedded that it seems unlikely that horses will ever be eliminated from farm life altogether.

The Marjawici Felicjanowcy

Every year in May or early June, about two thousand pilgrims from cities and towns as far away as two hundred and fifty miles gather in a tiny village in central Poland to celebrate the so-called Green Holidays. This festival, in which participants pray for Mary's help to bring about a successful harvest, is observed throughout all of Poland. Churches, houses, cottages, and farm buildings are decorated with branches of birch, ash, or fir. People wind through the fields, singing and chanting prayers for a good crop. After the procession, a special mass is held in the church.[19]

What is unique about the Green Holidays in this particular village is that it coincides with the yearly reunion of nearly the entire membership of an unusual religious group which split from the Roman Catholic church in the early twentieth century. On this day members of the group return to their mecca—the village where the group was founded and in which its leaders live today. Named after their founder, Maria Felicja Kozłowska, members are called the Marjawici Felicjanowcy. They do not believe in papal infallibility. Their leaders include married priests and bishops and women priests (69, 70) and bishops (71, 72, 73), who live together in a commune composed of several buildings in the village. The leaders call one another brother and sister.

In 1928 the Polish press reported so-called mystical marriages between nuns and priests in this group. These marriages were not considered by the group to be a sin against God. On the contrary they were said to fulfill spiritual needs because sexual contact was believed to help lead to mystical experiences. Hence, such marriages were considered not only acceptable but a duty fulfilling the will of the Holy Spirit. Children born of these unions were raised collectively in the commune. In the words of the co-founder of this group, Jan Maria Michael Kowalski, these children were believed to be the beginning of a "new and renewed human race, . . . cleansed of every blemish of sin and renewed in body and soul . . ."[20] Whether such mystical marriages exist today is a secret impenetrable by anyone outside the Marjawici Felicjanowcy.

Perhaps the most surprising fact about this group is that they regard their founder, Mama Felicja Kozłowska, as the spiritual wife of Christ. They say that such a wife was foretold in the the Bible: "And a great portent appeared in heaven, a woman clothed with the sun, with the moon under her feet, and on her head a crown of twelve stars" (Rev. 12:1, RSV). To the Marjawici Felicjanowcy this passage was fulfilled in the twentieth century by Mama Kozłowska's appearance on earth. Furthermore, they claim that Mama Kozłowska is a member of the Holy Trinity. On the altar in their church a black and white photograph of Mama Kozłowska hangs on the right side of Christ, surrounded by white flowers, and a picture of Mary, Mother of God, hangs on the left side (74). All day and all night someone is continually kneeling before this altar in prayer to Christ, his mother, and his spiritual bride.

Given the high esteem rendered to Mama Kozłowska by her followers, it is little wonder that festivities in her honor are included in the celebration of the Green

71

Holidays in this village, the site of our fifth journey. After a mass and a procession through a nearby park, the pilgrims gather around a podium behind which hangs a large colored portrait of Mama Kozłowska. With this portrait as a backdrop, bishops and priests give speeches and read poetry describing Mama Kozłowska's life and her efforts to redeem the world. A choir sings in her honor (75).

> Our mama,
> Queen of the world.
> People have awaited you for many years,
> Through you great grace was given to us.
> Have mercy on us,
> Have mercy,
> O God's chosen one.
>
> Full of saintliness,
> Full of compassion,
> O most holy mama,
> Beloved mother,
> God's chosen one,
> Pray for us.
> Pray for us.

Near the close of the festivities a speaker announces, "Now there will be a waltz in honor of the women bishops." A group of girls in white dresses with white flowered wreaths in their hair comes out onto the stage and dances a waltz to the music of a harmonica while sugar candies are tossed onto the podium. After the waltz there is a closing recitation about Mama Kozłowska. With that, the festivities end, and people depart for home.

The founder of this unusual group was born in 1862 into a family whose ancestors include Kazimierz Pułaski, the famous Polish general who fought in the American Revolution. When Felicja Kozłowska was of age, she became a Roman Catholic nun. While in her early twenties, one eye became blind so that, as she put it, she could see more deeply into the human soul with the one eye only. The power of that single eye was so penetrating that one of her nuns said, "It knew all the answers before they reached my lips."[21]

In 1887, at the age of twenty-five, Felicja Kozłowska founded a small nunnery called the Sisters of Saint Clara, whose members were to maintain a state of poverty and of purity of spirit and to engage in unceasing prayer before the altar of Christ. This group of five women was so poor that they had one coat and one pair of adequate shoes among them; so in winter they went to church by turns. They ate little food and were often cold.[22] Their most important spiritual activity was the adoration of the Eucharist.

In these early days, Felicja Kozłowska already had much charisma, and she inspired adoration even from novices older than herself. One of them says that when she met

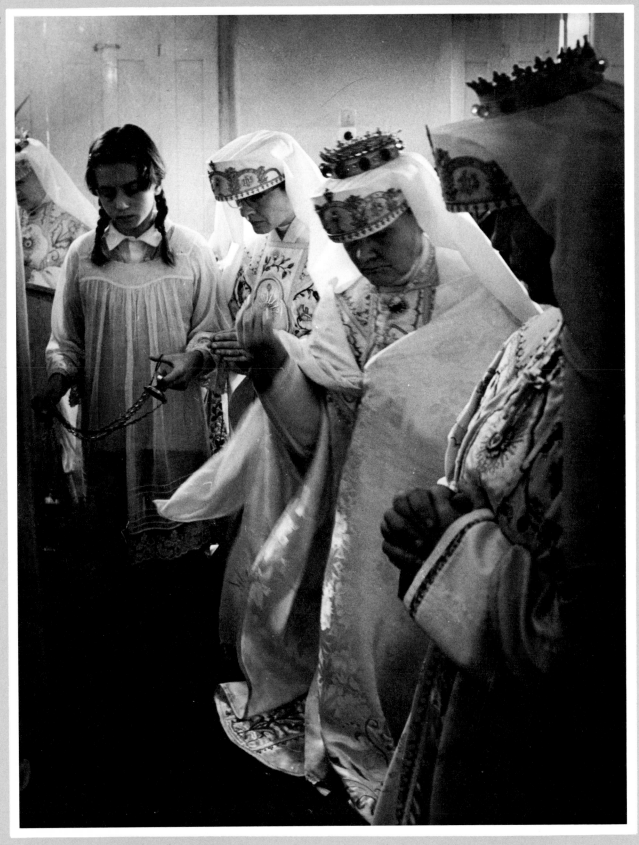

72

Felicja Kozłowska for the first time she felt compelled to kneel and call her, "My mother."[23]

Felicja Kozłowska became known for her feminist preachings. Women, she said, must learn how to look after themselves; husbands should not be their only raison d'être. The will of God and the will to work must go together.[24]

In 1893 Felicja Kozłowska had a miraculous vision in which she saw the downfall of the Catholic church, due primarily to the demoralization of the clergy. She describes the experience as follows:

> . . . I was suddenly detached from my senses and placed before the Majesty of God. Inconceivable luminosity suffused my soul and I was then shown the universal corruption of the world and the finality of time—the laxity of morals among the clergy and the sins committed by priests.
>
> I saw God's Justice aiming at the world to punish it and also his Mercy giving the doomed world its last chance of rescue in the Veneration of the Most Holy Sacrament and in Mary's Help. After a moment of silence the Lord spoke: "To spread this worship I want to see a congregation of priests under the name of Marjawici. Their motto is: All for the greater glory of God and for the veneration of the Most Holy Virgin Mary . . ."
>
> I was greatly astonished and began to rejoice, but the Lord spoke again, "For the present I give all this Work in your hands—you are to be its mistress and mother." Immediately I muttered, "Behold the handmaid of the Lord; be it unto me according to thy word."[25]

Felicja Kozłowska had several subsequent visions, or "understandings" as she came to call them, during which she was instructed how to save the world. According to those understandings, which she felt to be from Jesus Christ, people must take Mary, the Mother of God, as a model for their lives and must spread her worship throughout the world. Each person who followed this path was to call himself or herself a Marjawita, derived from the Latin *Maria vitae,* which means "the life of Mary." In Polish the plural of this name becomes *Marjawici.* Furthermore, according to Felicja Kozłowska, people must engage in continual adoration of the holy sacrament, day and night, and pray before the altar of Christ for the betterment of the world and an end to evil. Finally, people must become willing to help one another.

Felicja Kozłowska wrote down her ideas in a book which she called the *Work of Great Mercy.* She was convinced that these concepts would one day reign throughout the world. She intended her reforms to be adopted by the Roman Catholic church, and to bring this about she formed a group, originally priests dissatisfied with themselves and in search of spiritual guidance. Having heard about her visions, priests often came by riverboat to her pleasant house and garden in Płock, outside Warsaw. Typically, when a visiting priest would meet her face to face—or rather eye to eye—he would open his soul to her, feel waves of strength and peace radiating from her; at once all was understood, forgiven, and transformed. Then, bending on his knee, the priest would kiss Kozłowska's hand in acceptance of her spiritual direction.[26]

73

Eventually these grateful clergymen came to call her *Mateczka,* which means "Mama." One of these priests, Jan Maria Michael Kowalski, who previously smoked, overate, and played cards, described the experience of meeting Mama Kozłowska as one of having been reborn. About eight months after their first meeting, Mama Kozłowska visited Kowalski in Warsaw. He prostrated himself before her, and kissed the ground on which she was standing. She bade him to rise and told him that after communion that morning she had experienced a spiritual union with him; she also told him that there would be a separate heaven for Marjawici and that he would be near her in that heaven.[27] Kowalski later succeeded Mama Kozłowska as leader of the movement.

It was not long before the Marjawici ran into conflict with Pope Pius X. He first condemned Mama Kozłowska's idea of not collecting any money for religious services. When he heard about her plans to allow women to become priests and bishops as well as to endorse marriages between priests and nuns, he excommunicated Mama Kozłowska together with her co-worker Jan Kowalski and condemned her group.

That official action occurred in 1906, by which time the group had become a popular movement, numbering about one hundred thousand. Following the excommunication, the Marjawici were heavily persecuted. Fanatic Roman Catholics burned down their meeting houses, and when they met Marjawici on the street, they stripped them of their holy clothes and beat them. Sometimes bloody riots ensued. The Marjawici were easy to recognize because they wore ashen gray soutanes with a monstrance sewn in golden threads on the front.

Under pressure of this persecution, many returned to the Catholic church. However, the movement did not die and grew even stronger after Mama Kozłowska's death in 1921. Its members so honored their founder that they began to claim she was the spiritual wife of Christ and developed a cult around her. The Marjawici also became known for social welfare activities. According to statistics compiled in March, 1923, two years after Mama Kozłowska's death, the Marjawici had four boarding schools for orphans, forty-five kindergartens, thirteen homes for old people and invalids, four medical units, ten kitchens for the poor, thirty-two workshops, seven bakeries, three fire brigades, twenty-two farms, and twenty-five vegetable and fruit gardens.[28]

In 1924 marriages between priests and nuns were sanctioned among the Marjawici, and in 1928 women were allowed to become priests. The Marjawici believed that the church had undergone a great loss by restricting the functions of the priesthood to only one-half the human race. Henceforth women were to give communion and undertake all other functions of the priesthood. These changes caused an outpouring of articles in the Polish press ridiculing and mocking the Marjawici and accusing them of worshiping Mama Kozłowska on a higher level than Mary, of being an illegal cloister, of having contact with the Eastern Orthodox church, and of being a "crazy religion." Once again physical persecutions of the Marjawici ensued. For example, a boy of about twelve—urged on by a group

of hysterical women—whistled at and threw a stone at a Marjawici priestess as she walked through his village. Blood began to trickle over her eyelid. When at last she was able to continue on her way, she went up to the boy and touched him on the head, as if sensing his need of forgiveness.[29]

In 1935 a conflict arose among the Marjawici, dividing them into two factions. One side, which came to call itself the Marjawici Felicjanowcy, believed that confession should be made directly to God and not through a priest. This group also did away with holy water and fully accepted women priests. They recognized Mama Kozłowska as the wife of Christ and as a member of the Holy Trinity, believing that only through worship of her would the world become a better place. The second group, the Marjawici Płockie, returned to having confessions through a priest and to using holy water in their services. They did away with women priests and recognized Mama Kozłowska merely as the founder of a new religious group but not as the wife of Christ or a member of the Holy Trinity.

As a result of this dispute, the Marjawici Felicjanowcy broke away from the Marjawici Płockie and moved to another village. The Marjawici Płockie today number about twenty-five thousand, and near the grave of Mama Kozłowska they have a beautiful cloister whose entire interior is painted white. The Marjawici Płockie have come to vary little from the Roman Catholic church.

The Marjawici Felicjanowcy, to whom we paid a visit on our fifth journey, continue to differ radically with the Catholic church. They number about four thousand, seven hundred of whom live in the founding village. The rest are scattered throughout Poland.

During World War II many priests from both groups were taken to concentration camps. Throughout the war, Jews and priests of all kinds were the most heavily persecuted groups in Poland. A Marjawici priest who survived recalls that one punishment was to tie about twenty campmates to a cement roller and make them to pull it along. If one fell from exhaustion, the others were forced to keep going and roll over the fallen prisoner.

Today the priests and bishops of the Marjawici Felicjanowcy live a quiet life in their cloister. They are no longer persecuted. In fact, as part of their celebration of the Green Holidays they proudly recite poems recalling that only under the Polish People's Republic did the Marjawici church become legalized and the persecution cease.

The Marjawici accept no money for their religious services. To support themselves they run a model farm on which rye, wheat, and potatoes are grown and cows, pigs, and chickens are raised. They also draw income from their fine embroidery, which equals Japanese needlework in skill and precision. They make their own holy vestments, decorating them with flowers and patterns (71, 72). They also make and sell banners for trade guilds, such as barbers, carpenters, and bakers. These banners require several months of painstaking labor and sell for several thousand dollars each.

One of the most unusual examples of Marjawici embroidery is a miniature picture of

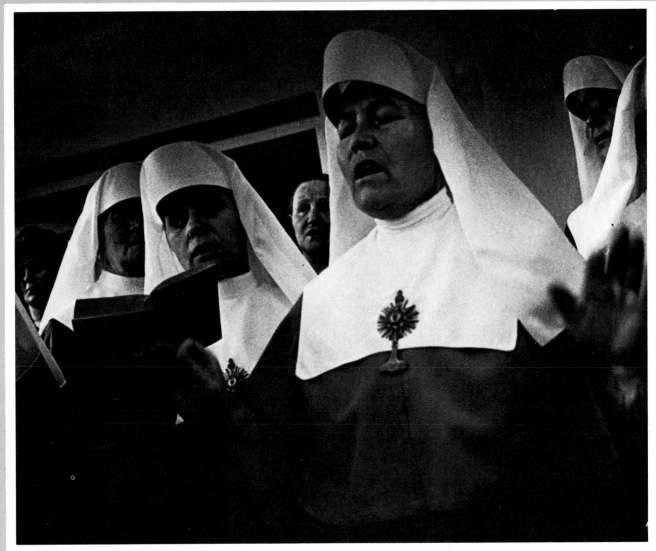

75

Mama Kozłowska which has been placed just below the golden monstrance in their church. This picture shows Mama Kozłowska on her deathbed, suffering from ascites, a very painful disease which causes the abdomen to swell to an enormous size.

Today the Marjawici cloister is a cultural center for the surrounding area. Many young peasant girls receive training in cooking and baking from the Marjawici nuns. Among the membership of the Marjawici Felicjanowcy are many highly educated people, some with masters' degrees and doctorates. As they speak of their religion, and particularly of their founder, Mama Felicja Kozłowska, their faces become flushed and tears come to their eyes.

The Funeral and Assumption of the Mother of God

No one knows how or where Mary, the mother of Jesus, died. The Bible tells us only that Jesus placed her in the care of the disciple John. John went to Patmos, but there is no indication that she accompanied him.

As a result of this factual vacuum, many stories evolved concerning the circumstances of Mary's death. According to the earliest legend, circulated in the fifth century, Mary died in Jerusalem and was attended by the disciples who were miraculously assembled. Her body was carried in a funeral procession, placed in a sepulchre, and then raised by the command of Jesus, when he appeared before the tomb with a band of angels who bore Mary straightaway into heaven, body and soul.

According to some versions, the angel Gabriel came and told Mary she would die within three days. With the exception of Thomas, the disciples were with her when she fell asleep. On the third day after her death, Thomas came to venerate her. When the disciples opened the tomb, she was gone. They concluded that she had been taken straight to heaven, body and soul, as Jesus had been.[30]

Most legends concerning Mary's death have in common the belief that her body did not decay and that soon after her burial it was reunited with her soul and taken up into heaven. Her death became known as the Dormition, or falling asleep, and the mysterious act of her being taken up into heaven, body and soul, became known as the Assumption.

As a liturgical feast, the Dormition of Mary was celebrated in the Byzantine Church as early as the end of the sixth century and was adopted by Rome during the seventh century. From its Western inception, the feast centered around Mary's bodily glorification, and thus by the end of the eighth century the title of the feast had been changed from the Dormition to the Feast of the Assumption. In the East the Dormition of Mary was retained and emphasized.[31] By the ninth century the Assumption of Mary had become a major festival and soon became the principal Marian festival although the doctrine of the corporeal assumption was not declared an article of faith by papal decree until 1950.[32]

The choice of August 15 for this celebration coincided with the European harvest season, and the feast also became known as Our Lady in Harvest. The spirit of Assumption Day is not only one of rejoicing over the triumphal union of Mary with her divine Son but of thanksgiving for the harvest. Mary is believed able to intercede favorably for abundant crops.[33] Even today, many Assumption shrines in Europe show Mary clothed in a robe covered with ears of grain.

Assumption Day is celebrated in a variety of ways throughout the Catholic and Eastern Orthodox world. In Hungary pageants and parades honor Mary as the "Great Lady of the Hungarians" as well as Jesus' mother. In Austria the faithful are led by a priest through fields and meadows as they sing prayers and hymns asking God's blessing on the harvest. In France a statue of Mary is carried in solemn procession through the cities and towns with great splendor and pageantry while church bells ring out and the faithful sing hymns in Mary's honor. The so-called Bowing Procession is held in rural sections outside

78

Rome. A statue of Mary is carried through the streets, symbolizing a journey to heaven. Under a gaily decorated arch of branches and flowers representing the gate of heaven, it is met by a statue of Christ. Both figures bow to each other three times. Then Christ leads his mother back to the parish church, symbolizing Mary's entrance into eternal glory. At the church the ceremony is concluded by a service of solemn benediction.[34] In Greece, where the Eastern Orthodox church predominates, this festival is usually celebrated at night. A large oblong icon of a supine Mary surrounded by the disciples is carried in procession around the church three times. Parishioners holding lighted candles follow and then proceed to the homes of the sick who touch the icon with their hands. It is believed that this will make them well.[35]

On this day in most Polish villages each family brings a harvest wreath of flowers and fruits to the church to be blessed. And in at least two Polish villages an unusual celebration called the Funeral and Assumption of the Mother of God, or the Funeral and Triumph of the Mother of God, takes place during this season. This celebration embraces the Dormition as well as the Assumption of Mary and the spirit of thanksgiving of the harvest season. A life-sized wooden statue of Mary lying in an open casket is carried in a funeral procession (76) to an above-ground grave, symbolizing her Dormition. Later a statue of a risen Mary is carried in procession to a chapel, representing her Assumption.

One of these celebrations takes place in the same town as the Holy Week Celebration of the Sufferings of the Lord. The event attracts about one hundred fifty thousand people. Another celebration occurs in a tiny village in the southeastern section of Poland, near the Russian border, and draws a pilgrimage of about ten to twenty thousand people.

This second village is the goal of our sixth journey. The celebration begins on August 11 and ends on Assumption Day, August 15.

Since no bus goes directly to this village from the nearest city, we travel the last twenty-five miles on foot, surrounded by companies of singing pilgrims who wind their way through hills and valleys. Finally we reach a hill called the Mount of Olives. From its peak we can see the village monastery on top of the next hill, its tin rooftops sparkling in the sunlight. As we pause to rest, a company of pilgrims arrives, their banners waving in the wind. When the church towers of the village become visible, they prostrate themselves in reverence (77) and remain in this position for several minutes of silent meditation. Birds call overhead, and the smell of newly mown hay fills the air.

The company rises, resumes their singing, and moves on toward the village. As their songs become an echo in the distance they are replaced by those of the next company, who likewise pause to prostrate themselves on the hill. In this second company we see an old man carrying a small brown suitcase and a black umbrella, teen-age boys with knapsacks slung over their backs, and old women with flowered kerchiefs tied at the back of their necks. Dusty sandals strap the wrinkled ankles of the elderly women. They carry their

belongings in cardboard boxes, in canvas bags tied with string, or in sheets and blankets slung over their backs.

As this second company leaves, we descend into the valley, cross the river, and begin to climb the steep hill to the village. Little knots of people are picnicking in the forests beside the road; they have left their banners hanging in the tree branches while they sit down to enjoy their food.

We climb the hill in the dusty wake of a car that whizzes by. A joyful melody pours from the car windows. It is only one of a parade of automobiles and motorcycles.

At last we arrive in the tiny village, composed of one main street and about twenty-five houses. As each company of singing pilgrims arrives, they proceed to the huge baroque church and prostrate themselves on the hard marble steps to the altar, where they receive a blessing from the priest. Then the pilgrims look for somewhere to lay down their belongings in order to reserve a place to sleep. There is no central organization for accommodations; there are no lists, no assignments. The pilgrims simply know what to do. Some pitch tents on the church grounds or in the fields. Others negotiate a place on a straw-covered cottage floor. Still others find places in the haylofts of the Franciscan monastery, an especially popular choice for groups of teenagers, families, and other pilgrims not traveling in companies.

As this village of seventy swells to twenty thousand, its single street becomes noisy and crowded. A bazaar which has been set up runs continually throughout the event, offering everything from silver crosses and rubber balls to cotton candy and cowboy hats. Young boys pull carts of tomatoes and pickles down the road, selling them or sometimes giving them away. For a small fee, local villagers dish out bowls of soup and cups of tea to the weary pilgrims.

About four in the afternoon the people gather at the church for the first of several processions during their four-day stay. The pilgrims are led by four young men dressed in black suits and about twenty young girls wearing white blouses, white gloves, and dark blue or white skirts. In their hands the girls carry golden robes with which they will dress the statue of Mary.

The group descends into a valley and moves towards a small chapel called the House of the Mother of God. The girls in white blouses enter and clothe a life-sized wooden figure of Mary with the golden robes (78). They place a golden crown on her head and a sceptre in her hand. The four black-suited pallbearers lift up the casket on which she lies, carry it out of the house, and stand in front of the chapel. The girls follow and surround the statue. A priest comes out onto the balcony of the chapel and delivers a sermon to the crowd standing or sitting on the hillside below. He warns people that in their struggle for material well-being they should not forget God.

After the sermon the pilgrims return to the church. The pallbearers carry Mary's

casket inside and place it under a canopy on an altar, where it lies in state for two days. Throughout these days, twelve young girls dressed in white with piously folded, white-gloved hands surround the statue and sing special hymns to Mary (79). Every hour another group of twelve girls comes to relieve the present group. A continual vigil is kept until about 10:30 each evening, when the church closes, and resumes at four the next morning.

At various times of day and evening pilgrims flow in and out of the church and go around the statue of Mary three times on their knees in meditation. As they move along, some hand Bibles, postcards, rosary beads, or plastic-framed pictures of Mary or Jesus to one of the girls. The girl touches the object to Mary's dress as a blessing, then hands it back.

By evening about twenty thousand pilgrims have arrived. After supper they bring their blankets and gather in the church courtyard under the arching trees to hear a Franciscan priest welcome them and inform them about where to get first aid and water. He also points out the location of the latrines and warns the people to beware of thieves; then he announces the program for the next few days.

After the priest's announcements, Italian films on the lives of Jesus and Mary are projected on the outside wall of the monastery. Then some young people bring their guitars out onto the church balcony and perform religious songs they have composed themselves. About midnight the crowd disperses to return to the sleeping areas. Candles can be seen glowing from inside the tents as some pilgrims keep vigil in song all night long.

At dawn the next morning a crowing rooster calls the people to six o'clock mass. Men and boys prop up jagged mirrors on the barn window ledges to shave. Pilgrims in the hayloft open up their satchels to take out bread and cheese for their breakfast. An old woman slices off a piece of bread and hands it to a young girl. In exchange the girl offers her a hard-boiled egg. An old man with a battered leather bag full of fresh plums from his farm shares them with the others. After breakfast everyone from the hayloft lines up at one of the cottages for a cup of morning tea.

After mass, people spend this second day in prayer, in confession, and in fellowship with one another. Behind the church a group of elderly women from various villages gather as they do every year at this festival. Standing in a circle they exchange news about their families, this year's good harvest, the price of shoes, and so forth.

Nearby a thirty-four-year-old worker who punches out seven hundred buttons an hour in a nearby factory sits on a log and listens to an old man tell about his experiences as a Nazi prisoner of war. It is this man's fifth year at the celebration, and he has brought along a young television repairman from his village. After conversing for about an hour, the three hike to the chapel of Mary Magdalene. There they encounter a company of pilgrims who are encircling the chapel three times on their knees. The old man, the button worker, and the television repairman get down on their knees and go around the chapel.

81

After the third time, the television repairman's knees begin to bleed a bit. He smiles and says, "Now I'll remember that I've been here."

His trials have not yet ended. Since this is his first year, he is obliged to walk backward down the hill from Mary Magdalene's chapel to the main church. The way is steep and full of rocks and trees, but he does not fall because the worker and the elderly man hold his arms and guide his steps. On the way down they meet others also going down the hill backward.

On the third day, August 13, the major procession takes place—Mary's funeral. Throngs of pilgrims gather at the church as the casket is brought out by four pallbearers. Wanting to be as near the statue as possible, people push and shove, and children climb on their parents' shoulders to see better.

Mary's bier is carried down the road. The singing pilgrims crowding the streets open a path for her, and villagers open their windows to look down on the procession (80) which continues for miles through forests and valleys to six different chapels (81). Most pilgrims travel with their companies. Those at the head of each group carry banners or wooden crosses. As they arrive at a particular chapel, they pause and gather around their leader (82) who leads in prayer. Then they move on toward the next chapel.

Like those at the pilgrimage to the Celebration of the Sufferings of the Lord, these leaders are chosen on the basis of moral character. They also usually have loud resonant voices, and as they sing, their voices echo throughout the valleys.

Some of their music dates from the nineteenth century when Poland was occupied by the Germans, Russians, and Austrians. Indicative of a suffering nation, these songs plea for freedom, something the people desired but were not allowed to write about in newspapers or even speak of in the streets. One of the songs goes as follows:

Ave Maria,
Mother of God.
We beseech you,
Holy Virgin,
With tears in our eyes,
With warm hearts—
Take pity on us.
Pity us,
Suffering people,
O Mother of God.
Bless us.
We fall down on our knees,
O Mother of God,
The whole world gathers unto you;
Your charity and help we wait.
Calvary mother, help us,
Mother, beloved.

82

Despite the seriousness of some songs, the atmosphere is joyful, more like a fair or a picnic (83) than a funeral. Indeed, the people are dressed as for a picnic (84, 85, 86). Teenagers wear bright shirts and colored paper-chain necklaces which they have bought at the bazaar. Most of the women wear cotton dresses. Young boys wear baseball caps, and many young girls wear wreaths of flowers in their hair.

One of the most dramatic moments occurs when Mary crosses the river (76). The pallbearers remove their shoes and socks, roll up their pant legs, and wade through the river (87–92), which is about thirty feet wide and knee deep.

After Mary has crossed the river, its waters are regarded as holy. People dip their hands in it and touch their faces and eyes;[36] they fill bottles to take home.

Not everyone has to wade through the river. Plank bridges on wagons span the water in about twelve places (93, 94). If one chooses to cross by bridge, one must pay a penny at the other side. ·

Finally the procession arrives at the Chapel of Mary's Grave. The casket is carried inside and laid in a grave on a platform raised above the ground (95). One of the priests takes off Mary's golden robes and replaces them with white ones. Girls enter the chapel and toss the wreaths they have been wearing onto the casket. A priest comes out on the balcony and gives a sermon to the thousands of pilgrims gathered below.

After the sermon the people walk in procession to the main church. Tired from their twenty-five mile journey up and down steep hills, they share the evening meal in tents, haylofts, or cottages.

On the fourth day, the pilgrims again rise at dawn, this time to walk the twenty-four Stations of the Cross, which are also built on this hilly terrain. There is no general gathering of people; instead, each company makes its own way. Young boys wear wreaths of branches on their heads to resemble crowns of thorns.

At each chapel the company leaders speak about the particular stage in Christ's passion and its meaning for today. At the Chapel of Pontius Pilate's Palace a stone canopied pathway leads to the balcony, the scene of Jesus' trial. The pilgrims enter this chapel and go down the steps of that pathway backward on their knees, kissing each step. When they reach the bottom, they lie in a cross on the ground outside and meditate silently for a few moments. As they reach the Chapel of the Crucifixion, several women wipe tears from their eyes.

It is Assumption Eve. At 10:00 P.M. the pilgrims carrying lighted candles gather at the church (96) and walk to the Chapel of the Assumption. Leading the procession are four black-suited pallbearers carrying an upright statue of Mary with a crown on her head and a sceptre in her hand. Wrapped in blankets to keep out the chill evening air, the pilgrims sing songs in honor of Mary.

At the chapel they sit on blankets and listen to a priest give a short sermon. Afterwards, gathering their blankets around them, the pilgrims return to their sleeping quarters.

83

Since this is the last night of the holiday, havoc breaks out among some of the young people in the haylofts. They put green toothpaste on one another's feet, noses and hands, and one fellow rubs coal all over a young girl's face. With her hands covering her face in embarrassment, the girl runs to the sink in the monastery, but the cold water is of no avail in removing the coal's blackness.

The next morning people pack up their belongings and prepare for the journey home. The old man in the hayloft who shared his plums now carefully wraps his blanket around a clay statue of Mary which has been blessed in the church. He searches the ground for a piece of string with which to tie his bundle. The old women who spent time gossiping about the price of shoes once again gather behind the barn and hug each other good-by. One says, "May God grant us the strength to meet here again next year." The young girl who exchanged an egg for a slice of bread asks the old woman, "How do you feel?" to which she replies, "Like a fairy tale."

With songs on their lips the pilgrims wind their way out of the village and head toward home where they will be welcomed at their churches.

As companies of singing pilgrims walk through the streets of the nearest city, people lean out the windows and wave to them. From many window ledges, embroidered cloths and pictures of Mary hang in honor of Assumption Day. A company of pilgrims goes to the station to await the next train to their village. As they sit on the bench, still singing songs in Mary's honor, a young woman turns to a member of the company and says, "I hear one walks long miles at that festival. It must be very tiring." The pilgrim, a seventy-year-old woman who has been coming since her childhood, smiles and answers, "You don't really feel the tiredness. There's such an atmosphere."

According to a priest who resides in this village and witnesses the pilgrims each year, these several days spent engaging oneself body and soul in worship often awaken a resolution to change one's life for the better. The priest especially stresses the importance of making a sincere confession and taking Holy Communion, of listening to sermons on the life of Jesus and his mother, and of sharing fellowship with people full of faith. According to him, many young priests and nuns attribute their calling to experiences at this pilgrimage.

The pilgrims who come to celebrate Mary's Funeral and Assumption are primarily from villages within about a two-hundred-mile radius. Most are small independent farmers who give up some of their vacation time to make the journey. Many come on foot the entire way.

This monumental event is to some extent organized by the Franciscan monks who reside in this village, but most of the responsibility falls upon Szymon, a porter at the Jagiellonian University in Cracow and a member of the Archbrotherhood of the Sufferings of the Lord (see chapter 2). From among two of the larger companies of pilgrims, Szymon selects the pallbearers and the young girls who keep vigil around Mary's statue. He also

buys the robes for Mary each year, paying for them primarily out of his own pocket, although contributions from Polish Americans help somewhat.

Now about seventy, Szymon has organized the Funeral and Assumption of the Mother of God since his youth. Even during the Nazi occupation, when all such celebrations were forbidden, he insisted on carrying out this tradition. He and about a hundred other people walked the path of Mary's funeral. They did not carry the heavy casket or the banners; instead, they carried just the statue of Mary. Szymon held her head, and a friend supported her feet. As the Germans approached, the celebrants scattered into the forests. In 1945, the village was directly on the front. Szymon held the procession with only five people.

This village and the celebration of Mary's funeral were founded in the mid-seventeenth century by Andrzej Maksymilian Fredro (1620–79), a wealthy aristrocrat, a castellan of Lwów, and one of Poland's outstanding seventeenth-century writers.[37] Fredro founded this village in response to the moral devastation in his country after years of cruel wars with the Cossaks and Swedes. He was looking for a means to elevate the people spiritually and to dissolve their hatred and desire for revenge.

Fredro decided that the best means to achieve this would be to place before people's eyes Christ, who asked his Father to forgive even his executioners. Fredro chose this place because its hills, valleys, and river reminded him of similar terrain in and around Jerusalem. At first he built a small wooden church and twenty-four wooden chapels, later adding six chapels representing stages in Mary's death and burial.

In 1669 Fredro gave the church and chapels to the Franciscan monks, with the understanding that they would lead people along the paths of the Sufferings of Christ and of the death of Mary, explain what each chapel meant, and encourage people to lead a Christian life.

A few years after all the chapels had been built, a miraculous picture[38] of the Mother of God was brought here from Russia. From that moment larger and larger crowds came in pilgrimage. The church soon proved too small; so in 1770 a new and larger church and new chapels were begun, this time out of stone. Thousands of wagons of stone were lugged up the steep mountain, and after five years the church and the chapels were completed. It is these buildings we see today.

Before World War II, as many as one hundred thousand people came to this place to celebrate the Funeral and Assumption of the Mother of God, including many Ruthenians and Ukrainians. Today the Soviet border, just a few miles from the village, cuts off the vast majority of former participants.

86

93

96

The Funeral and Triumph of the Mother of God

98

144

In the village where Holy Week events are reenacted, as presented in Chapter Three, Mary's funeral and assumption are celebrated with great pomp and majesty. Costumed folk groups from nearly all regions of Poland participate (97, 98); brass bands play funeral marches (99–103); newlyweds come in their wedding clothes (104). A group of virgin cleaning women from Cracow come in white dresses with white flowers in their hands and white veils streaming down their backs (105, 106). Schoolgirls arrive in short white dresses with white floral wreaths in their hair (107, 108). A group of older women wear long white tunics with white sashlike veils placed over their heads and across their shoulders (109); these women carry white ribbons and flowers in one hand and satchels of food in the other. Some carry large pictures of Mary (110); many carry flowers and wreaths.

Some companies of pilgrims come several days before the celebration to walk the path of the Sufferings of the Lord, to visit with old friends from previous years, and to mill about the bazaar. At this festival the bazaar includes a large carousel with wooden horses which people can ride.

This splendid event attracts about one hundred fifty thousand pilgrims. It is much better known than the Celebration of the Sufferings of the Lord (see chapter 3). The celebration begins at 5:00 P.M. on August 18 at a chapel called the House of the Mother of God which is situated in the forests about two miles from the main church. We gather at this chapel with thousands of other pilgrims for our seventh journey. Most have come in companies (111), but unlike the celebration in the previous chapter, the people do not stay in companies; instead, they form a massive procession which stretches for nearly three miles. At the head are the leaders of all the pilgrimages. The leaders stand together creating a forest of crosses followed by a sea of banners (112). Next come the various folk groups and bands, followed by the mass of pilgrims. Each group has a specially designated place in the procession; all stand in silence waiting to begin.

At last a life-sized wooden statue of Mary (113) emerges from the chapel. She is resting on a casket decorated in baroque style, with wreaths of flowers at her feet and a crown on her head. Above her is a velvet brocade canopy. Four young men carry the statue onto a podium which has been erected in front of the chapel.

Unlike the celebration of Mary's funeral on our last journey, here there is no ceremonial dressing of Mary. A Gothic statue with painted-on clothing is used; no one knows where it came from.

Following the casket come the disciples of Jesus played by the same men who portrayed these roles at the Celebration of the Sufferings of the Lord. While the casket, pallbearers, and disciples stand on the podium, a mass and a sermon are given by one of the Bernardine priests. His words are amplified over a loudspeaker so that they can be heard for miles around. They are also piped into the main church in the town, enabling those who cannot walk in procession to listen.

After the mass and the sermon, the young men bearing the statue of Mary take their

places just behind the crosses and the banners. The disciples follow close behind. When all have found their places, the signal is given to begin.

As this enormous procession moves through the forests and valleys, the bands play funeral marches, each group a different tune. The folk groups sing when the bands rest. A rather somber, dignified mood predominates. The procession pauses several times in front of chapels, at each of which a sermon is given.

As night falls, the procession comes aglow with the lights of thousands of candles; nearly every person carries a candle in his hand. The few houses scattered in the forests are also illumined, so the people have no problem reading their handbooks of songs and prayers.

At about 8:00 P.M. the first pilgrims arrive at the grave of the Mother of God. It is an above-ground crypt located inside a baroque church on a small hill. The bands stop playing; the people stop singing. In silence and with great dignity the four pallbearers enter the chapel and place the casket on the grave while crowds of pilgrims squeeze into the church to watch.

Some pilgrims remain at this chapel in prayerful vigil all night while others return to their sleeping quarters. Many people sleep in the church, in haylofts, or on straw-covered cottage floors. Most of the folk groups and bands rent rooms in private homes or in the single hotel.

At six o'clock the next morning the festivities resume. Once again, the various groups gather near the Chapel of the Grave of the Mother of God. From the church emerge the four pallbearers carrying a three-foot high statue of a risen Mary (114) with a crown on her head and her hands folded in prayer. The pallbearers take their place in the procession, with the disciples following close behind. Once again the bands strike up—this time joyful tunes. People sing as they climb the hill to the main church. Here the pallbearers place the statue on a decorated altar. Trumpets announce this triumphant moment, and a choir of monks sings beautiful songs in Mary's honor. A mass and a sermon are given by two cardinals, Stefan Kardynał Wysinski and Karol Kardynał Wojtyła (115).

Then the tremendous crowd breaks up. The musical instruments are put away, costumes are packed into suitcases, and the pilgrims rejoin their companies, everyone gradually leaving for home. The town becomes quiet once again.

The first celebration of the Funeral and Triumph of the Mother of God—as this festival is officially called—took place in 1632. Little about its early history is known, but it is believed to have taken place every year since that date. During those early days a miraculous picture of Mary was brought to the church.

With the exception of loudspeakers, wristwatches, blue jeans, and cars, this event is believed to have changed very little since its origin. Like the Celebration of the Sufferings of the Lord, it is organized by the Bernardine monks who have resided there since the seventeenth century. And, as is true for the Celebration of the Sufferings of the Lord, the

person mainly responsible for this event is Father Augustyn Chadam, who has been in charge of both events since the end of World War II. Chadam meets with the leaders of the various groups when they arrive and assigns them places in the procession. Through his efforts, groups which might otherwise have died out with time have been encouraged to maintain their traditions.

In a tiny house in the woods behind the Chapel of Pontius Pilate's Palace lives a hermit (116), one of about a dozen religious hermits (117) who participate in the Funeral and Triumph of Mary. His house is composed of two rooms, each about five by nine feet (118). He sleeps and cooks in one room and offers the other room to guests. In each room a casket serves as a bed.

Living very simply, this hermit eats mostly bread, water, fruit, vegetables, eggs, and cheese. He earns his simple food by cleaning the chapels and church in the town and by tending the monastery's cows and the donkey on which Jesus enters Jerusalem on Palm Sunday. He accepts no money for his services; he is merely given his little house and food by the Bernardine monks.

When asked if he's a sad person, or a pessimist, a warm smile crosses his face, and he answers, "Why, God asked us to be happy. I have a lot of optimism inside me, and happiness" (119).

The precise origins of the Funeral and Assumption of the Mother of God and the Funeral and Triumph of the Mother of God are unknown. In some ways both are similar to pre-Christian Slavic celebrations. In those days in the Slavic lands at the beginning of summer, a large figure representing the Vegetation Spirit was enclosed in a coffin and carried through the streets attended by mourning women or singing maidens. Then the figure, usually made of straw, was burned, buried, or thrown into a river. In some cases it was revived and carried back to the town in a spirit of rejoicing.[39] Speculation that the celebrations of Mary's funeral and assumption descended from such observances finds support when we consider that among Polish peasants Mary is traditionally believed to give life and support to nature and to man; she is believed to help warm the air, open the earth, and reanimate dormant vegetation.[40]

The scenarios of these celebrations also contain elements found in some medieval dramas about the death and coronation of Mary. These plays were usually performed, not on Assumption Day, but as part of the Corpus Christi cycle.[41] The rituals also have characteristics in common with the legends mentioned in the last chapter.[42] Of particular

interest is the gathering of the disciples found in the celebration described in this chapter and in most of the plays and legends.

Whatever their origins, the enthusiasm with which both celebrations are carried out is closely tied to the enormous role Mary plays in the life of Polish peasants. In Poland more holidays honor Mary in the course of the year than any of the other saints, and more churches are named for her than for any other heavenly figure. One thousand fifty miraculous pictures of Mary are venerated throughout the country. The picture at Częstochowa mentioned at the outset of this book is known throughout the entire Catholic world.

In the peasant's hierarchy, Mary occupies a place second only to her divine Son. She is regarded as a mother to man as well as to God. Because of her tenderness, she is appealed to on behalf of the weak, the sick, the innocent, and those embarking on dangerous missions, such as soldiers going to war. Women feel that the Virgin Mary is their special friend and pray to her when approaching childbirth.

In Poland Mary is the heroine of countless popular legends, always as the benefactor of the weak, the oppressed, the burdened, and the lost. She is often referred to as the Protectress.[43]

109

119

The Transfiguration of Jesus Christ

Often in life when we encounter a problem too big for our own strength, we may turn to a friend, a neighbor, a doctor. Every year on August 18, about twelve thousand people of the Eastern Orthodox faith gather from all over Poland to bring their deepest problems directly to God. They make a cross out of wood and sometimes write their request on it. Then they pick up their cross, together with food and prayerbooks, and come to a holy mountain in the northeastern section of Poland.

On this mountain stands a wooden church with peacefully curved onion dome towers shaded by a forest of pine trees (120). Surrounding the church in a horseshoe are several hundred wooden crosses, and just beyond is a graveyard. Several yards from the church one finds another smaller church and a wooden building houses about ten Eastern Orthodox nuns. Aside from the nunnery, there is no sign of human life for miles around. Frogs croak in the nearby swamps, and flocks of storks fly overhead.

This holy mountain is the goal of our eighth and final journey. As we stand by the church, we see hundreds of arriving pilgrims (121). A father carries a cross on his back so large that it rests on the shoulders of his wife and daughter as well. Together they climb the last few steps up the mountain. An old woman with the experience of childbirth, war, and many harvests engraved into her aged face walks stooped under the weight of her heavy cross. An old man with a long beard carries a small cross under his arm. Farther down the road, horses splash their way through mud puddles as they draw wagons of pilgrims up the hill.

As the pilgrims climb the last steps of the mountain, they sing prayerful songs in Old Church Slavonic, White Russian, Russian, Polish, and various dialects. Most of these people are White Russians who live in Polish villages; some Ruthenians and a few Ukrainians also take part.

The singing pilgrims are welcomed by the constant gonging of the church bells which can be heard for miles around. Occasionally these peaceful sounds are punctuated by the noisy motors of arriving cars and motorcycles. Some cars bear crosses strapped to the roofs. They park a few hundred yards from the church.

Each worshiper comes with a particular request in mind. Some ask for more love in their family, for the unity of Christians, for the welfare of the patriarch; others petition for the well-being of their wives, or for the return of their child to the faith. One cross reads, "Lord God, turn me away from drunkenness and immorality." Perhaps the most frequent request is for family health.

When the pilgrims arrive with their crosses, they ask one of the many priests to perform a ceremony as they plant their crosses in the ground. Each pilgrim digs a hole, wraps a thin white cloth around the part of the cross to be planted, and pushes it into the soil (122). As he does so, the priest chants a prayer and sprinkles holy water on the cross with a brushlike dropper, making the sign of the cross with the brush.

The pilgrim remains by the cross for a time and prays (123) before going to look for

a place to sleep and wait for the celebration of the Transfiguration of Jesus Christ.[44]

The celebrants come with a faith that their requests will be answered because they believe the mountain to be holy, so holy that the pine trees beside the church have grown into an arch, as if to protect the building from storms. The holiness of this place was most dramatically demonstrated 266 years ago when it was the site of a great miracle.

At that time a cholera epidemic raged throughout the region, attacking people of all ages, positions, and nationalities. Thousands died, and mass graves were dug and filled. The epidemic led to great panic, and people of all faiths prayed continuously, but nothing seemed to deter the disease. One night an old man in a village hit by the epidemic dreamed that he saw a Byzantine icon of Mary telling him to gather people and go to a particular mountain. There they would be cured, and the epidemic would end.

The old man related his dream to an Eastern Orthodox priest who collected all the people in his village who had enough strength left to walk. Together they began their long journey on foot, making their way through forests, swamps, and hills as the priest led prayers. Many fell dead along the way, but the rest kept going.

Finally they reached the top of the mountain; all who made it were cured. As the story of this miracle spread, masses of people from miles around gathered and went to the mountain to be healed. Shortly thereafter the epidemic ended.

From that time on, the place was called the Holy Mountain, and a small wooden chapel was built on its peak. Every year thousands of people came in pilgrimage to give thanks for the end of the epidemic. Gradually they began to carry crosses with them and bring new requests to God. Thus, the thousands of crosses surrounding the church represent generations of prayers (124).

At some point in the history of this sacred place the commemoration of the Transfiguration of Jesus Christ intermingled with the bringing of the crosses. At about 6:00 P.M. on August 18, the ritual begins. An almost continual service takes place in front of the church, chanted by metropolitans, bishops, priests, and deacons from various regions throughout Poland.

As these leaders emerge from the church in their gold mitres and long green and gold satin robes (125, 126), the people crowd around them. The service does not take place on a raised platform but directly among the people. The priests chant, and a deacon swings the incense container among the crowd.

During the service, some priests hear confession off to one side of the church (127). Hundreds of people line up to acknowledge their non-Christian deeds and to ask forgiveness. Those who have made their confession proceed to the front of the church where they receive communion from a golden cup in which the bread and the wine are mixed. These elements are offered on a single long, golden spoon which is placed directly in the people's mouths. After receiving Communion, the people kiss the cup and both wrists of the priest.

One priest gives a sermon, during which he speaks of the lost brothers in the East, now sealed off from participation in this ritual by the Soviet border. Tears come to the eyes of some who listen.

Throughout the service there is much activity in and around the church. People enter, kiss the icons, and kneel to pray before them. On this day all the icons are decorated with evergreens. There are icons of Mary, of the twelve disciples, and of the saints, many the work of Stalony Dobrzanski, a contemporary artist. Dobrzanski also painted hundreds of pictures of saints directly on the walls and ceilings of the church.

At the front of the church is a large cut-out icon of Christ. Two old women tie finely embroidered cloths around this icon and kneel to pray. Another old woman goes about the church refilling each lamp with olive oil she has brought in her little sack. Other people light thin yellow wax candles and place them in brass holders on tables and pray. Each candle represents a request to God; as the candles burn, they incline toward one another.

Behind the church more people light candles and place them on a small wooden table. As dusk falls, the glow of candlelight touches the crosses, medals, and pictures of saints and of Mary which people have placed on the table. A priest blesses these objects by sprinkling them with holy water from a large broomlike brush. Nearby stand several women with handkerchiefs full of apples; the priest sprinkles the fruit with holy water.

One part of the service is a procession three times around the church. At the head of the procession are the priests (128); behind them celebrants carry a large icon with Mary on one side and a saint on the other. The choir follows singing beautiful songs; then come the crowds. Many fall to the ground in prayerful ecstasy and follow the icon around the church on their knees, their heads bowed in reverence. Some carry tiny children as they make their way around the church.

After circling the church three times, the procession goes to the cemetery to recite prayers for the dead which are so moving that many shed tears as they listen. The following is typical:

> O God of spirits, and of all flesh, who has trampled down Death, and overthrown the Devil, and given life unto they world: Do thou, the same Lord, give rest to the souls of thy departed servants, in a place of brightness, a place of verdure, a place of repose, whence all sickness, sorrow and sighing have fled away. Pardon every transgression which they have committed, whether by word, or deed, or thought. For thou are a good God and lovest mankind; because there is no man who liveth and sinneth not: for thou only art without sin, and thy righteousness is to all eternity, and thy word is true.[45]

About midnight the priests return to the church and continue offering liturgy all night long. Some of the liturgy takes place inside the church (129), and people enter to participate. There are no chairs; those who grow tired simply doze on the floor or on the stairway leading to the second story.

Outside, flames rise from a pile of wood. Old crosses which had fallen down and

begun to rot are being burned. Enough new ones have been brought this year that the old ones are not missed.

Some people slip away into the meadows and forests for a few hours sleep. They wrap their blankets around them to keep out the night chill.

Groups of people keep vigil all night long among the wooden crosses surrounding the church (130). They gather in little circles and place a candle in the center. By its flickering light they sing from old, yellow-paged song books. The moaning, eerie tones are broken from time to time by the whispering of the turning pages. Occasionally the people gather their blankets around themselves and doze against the crosses (131, 132).

As the first rays of dawn replace the candlelight and moonlight many continue to sing (133). Some, however, close their books and reach into their satchels for food. They spread soft cheese on bread and peel hard-boiled eggs. Those who are going to communion that morning refrain from eating. They sit and wait for the mass to begin (134).

About 8:00 A.M. the main mass commences. By this time about twelve thousand people have converged on the Holy Mountain. After the service another procession around the church takes place (135); it is similar to the one the night before. Once again, people fall to their knees in prayerful ecstasy (136). As they follow the icon around the church, their knees wear a path in the ground.

After the procession, the crowd gradually breaks up. Before they leave, many people gather down the road from the church around a well of mineral water, surrounded by a blue wooden railing. Arching over the railing is a metal dome with an Orthodox cross on top. The people dip their hands into the well waters and drink freely. They touch their eyes, their cheeks, their legs. They believe that this water will improve their health; indeed, scientists have substantiated this claim.

While some people gather at the well, others mill about the bazaar, looking for a souvenir. Those who depart by car head for the parking lot. Those who have come by horse-drawn wagon feed their horses with oats before beginning the journey home (137, 138).

127

133

136

Notes

1. Harvey Cox, *The Feast of Fools* (Cambridge: Harvard University Press, 1969), p. 7.

2. Sula Benet, *Song, Dance, and Customs of Peasant Poland* (New York: Roy Publishers), p. 25.

3. In the late eighteenth century, Poland was partitioned among three empires—Russian, Prussian, and Austro-Hungarian. Poland did not exist again as an independent nation until 1918.

4. The English publication is Jerzy Peterkiewicz's, *The Third Adam* (London: Oxford University Press, 1975). The bibliography contains a list of publications in Polish about the Marjawici. It does not mention Andrzej Tokarczyk, *Trzydzieści Wyznań* (Warsaw: Wydawnictwo Książka i Wiedza, 1971) which contains information about the Marjawici on pp. 209–26.

5. For example, Adam Bujak became a member of the Archbrotherhood of the Sufferings of the Lord and waited an entire year before taking a single picture.

6. Częstochowa, a city in south central Poland, is famous for its possession since 1382 of Our Lady of Częstochowa, the most well-known icon in Poland. Tradition says this icon was painted by St. Luke, but it is believed to be of ninth-century Greek origin. It is housed on Jasna Góra (the Hill of Light) above the city in a basilica which is the most renowned shrine in Central Europe. After this monastery withstood the siege of antipapal Swedes in 1655, Our Lady of Częstochowa was acclaimed "Queen of Poland" in 1656 and became a symbol of Polish nationalism and religious liberty. In commemoration of this event, every year about a million Poles come in pilgrimage to this place. H. M. Gillett, "Częstochowa," *New Catholic Encyclopedia,* Vol. 4 (New York: McGraw-Hill Book Co., 1967), p. 607, prepared by an editorial staff at the Catholic University of America, Washington, D.C.

7. Marguerite Ickis, *The Book of Festivals and Holidays the World Over* (New York: Dodd, Mead and Co., 1970), pp. 19, 20; see also *Encyclopedia Britannica,* The Macropedia 7, William Benton, Publisher (Chicago: Encyclopedia Britannica, Inc.), p. 199.

8. Sergius Bulgakov, *The Orthodox Church* (London: Centenary Press, 1935), p. 158.

9. The Roman Missal, *Lectionary for Mass* (New York: Catholic Book Publishing Co.), p. 801.

10. K. A. Heinrich Kellner, *Heortology: A History of the Christian Festivals from their Origin to the Present Day* (London: Kegan Paul, Trench, Trubner and Co., Ltd., 1908), p. 94.

11. M. Korduba, "The Reign of John Casimir: Part I 1648–54," and W. Tomkiewicz, "The Reign of John Casimir: Part II 1654–68," ed. W. F. Reddaway, *The Cambridge History of Poland,* vol. 1 (Cambridge: Cambridge University Press, 1956), pp. 502–31.

12. Some events which in the Bible take place at times other than Holy Week are also included, for example, Jesus' meeting with Mary Magdalene.

13. Each scene in the Celebration of the Sufferings of the Lord is followed by a sermon of up to twenty minutes. Most sermons are given by priests who reside in the Bernardine monastery in the town. Some are given by guest priests. The priests speak about the need for peace in the family and in the world, about the need for people to behave kindly toward one another, about Catholicism in Polish history, about the meaning of the particular stage in the Sufferings of the Lord, and so forth. The sermons serve to break up the intensity of the drama. To avoid monotony, these sermons will not be further mentioned in the descriptions of the major scenes in the Celebration of the Sufferings of the Lord.

14. A total of twenty-four scenes are enacted. Only the most significant are presented here. These include the traditional fourteen stations in the Way of the Cross.

15. Specifically, according to Luke 22:63–65.

16. Although this photograph was taken at the Chapel of the Crucifixion on another holiday, we nevertheless felt it an appropriate concluding picture for the story of Christ's passion.

17. The Bernardine monks were established by Saint Jan Kapistran of Cracow in 1453. In their early days the Bernardines were comprised of professors and scholars from the Jagiellonian University in Cracow. Today's Bernardine monks work in their own country and abroad, devoting much time to scholarly work. They have outposts in England, Argentina, and in the United States. For several years they have engaged in mission work among the Africans in the Republic of Zaire along the Congo River.

18. Benet, *Song, Dance, and Customs,* pp. 49–50.

19. Ibid., p. 67.

20. Peterkiewicz, *Third Adam,* p. 77.

21. Ibid., p. 8.

22. Ibid., p. 9.

23. Ibid., p. 10.

24. Ibid., p. 8.

25. Ibid., p. 10.

26. Ibid., p. 14.

27. Ibid., p. 28.

28. Ibid., p. 56.

29. Ibid., p. 3.

30. Father George Cheremeteff, personal communication.

31. D. F. Hickey, "Dormition of the Virgin," *New Catholic Encyclopedia,* p. 1017.

32. E. O. James, *Seasonal Feasts and Festivals* (New York: Barnes and Noble, Inc., 1961), p. 237.

33. Ibid.

34. Francis. X. Weiser, *Handbook of Christian Feasts and Customs* (New York: Harcourt, Brace and Co., 1952), p. 289.

35. A. Yoanidis-Haliasos, personal communication.

36. In some countries on Assumption Day people actually bathe in natural waters to receive a blessing: "An ancient custom in England, Ireland and sections of the European continent is the traditional bathing in oceans, rivers, and lakes on August 15 ('Our Lady's Health Bathing') to obtain or preserve good health through her intercession on whose great feast all water in nature is considered especially blessed" (Weiser, *Handbook,* p. 292).

37. Czesław Miłosz, *The History of Polish Literature* (Toronto, Ontario: Macmillan Co., Collier-Macmillan Canada, Ltd., 1969), p. 148.

38. A miraculous picture in the Catholic tradition is a painting which is an object of veneration because people praying before it to the person it represents have been known to receive miracles. These miracles are said to come, not from the painting itself, but through the intercession of the portrayed holy figure. That figure intercedes because of the faith of the person praying. The most famous miraculous picture in Poland is that at Częstochowa (see fn. 6). Father D. Frederick Helfrich, personal communication.

39. Jessie L. Weston, *From Ritual to Romance* (New York: Doubleday, 1957), p. 53.

40. Benet, *Song, Dance, and Customs,* p. 66.

41. James, *Seasonal Feasts,* p. 266. Two sources in English on the medieval plays on the Assumption of Mary are Brother Cornelius Luke, *The Role of the Virgin Mary in the Coventry, York, Chester and Townley Cycles* (Washington, D.C.: Catholic University of America, 1933), pp. 107–10; and J. S. Purvis, *The York Cycle of Mystery Plays* (London: S.P.C.K., 1957), pp. 354–72.

42. A source on the legends of Mary's death and assumption is R. L. P. Milburn, *Early Christian Interpretations of History* (London: Adam and Charles Black, 1954), pp. 161–92, appendix.

43. Benet, *Song, Dance, and Customs,* pp. 74–76.

44. The Transfiguration is a feast which commemorates Jesus' revelation of his divinity to Peter, James, and John on Mt. Tabor (Matthew; 7:1–13, Mark 2: 2–13, and Luke 9: 28–36). This holiday was extended throughout the universal church in 1457 by Callistus III. Felician A. Foy, editor, *The 1976 Catholic Almanac* (Huntingdon, Indiana, Our Sunday Visitor, Inc., 1975), p. 299.

45. Isabel Florence Hapgood, *The Service Book of the Holy Orthodox Catholic Apostolic Church* (New York: Syrian-Antiochian Orthodox Archdiocese of New York and North America, 1965), p. 565.

Bibliography

Benet, Sula. *Song, Dance, and Customs of Peasant Poland.* New York: Roy Publishers.

Bulgakov, Sergius. *The Orthodox Church.* London: Centenary Press, 1935.

Buttrick, George Arthur. *The Interpreter's Dictionary of the Bible.* New York: Abingdon Press, 1962.

Cox, Harvey. *The Feast of Fools.* Cambridge: Harvard University Press, 1969.

Foy, Felician A., editor. *The 1976 Catholic Almanac.* Huntingdon, Indiana: Our Sunday Visitor, Inc., 1975.

Hastings, James, ed. *The Encyclopedia of Religion and Ethics.* New York: Scribner's Sons., 1925.

James, E. O. *The Cult of the Mother Goddess.* London: Thames and Hudson, 1959.

————. *Seasonal Feasts and Festivals.* New York: Barnes and Noble, Inc., 1961.

Kellner, K. A. Heinrich. *Heortology: A History of the Christian Festivals from their Origin to the Present Day.* London: Kegan Paul, Trench, Trubner and Co., Limited, 1908.

Luke, Brother Cornelius. *The Role of the Virgin Mary in the Coventry, York, Chester and Townley Cycles.* Washington, D.C.: The Catholic University, 1933.

Milburn, R. L. P. *Early Christian Interpretations of History.* London: Adam and Charles Black, 1954.

Miłosz, Czesław. *The History of Polish Literature.* Toronto-Ontario: The Macmillan Company, Collier-Macmillan Canada, Ltd., 1969.

Peterkiewicz, Jerzy. *The Third Adam.* London: Oxford University Press, 1975.

Purvis, J. S. *The York Cycle of Mystery Plays.* London: S.P.C.K., 1957.

Reddaway, W. F., ed. *The Cambridge History of Poland.* Cambridge: Cambridge University Press, 1956.

Smith, Huston. *The Religions of Man.* New York: Harper and Row, Publishers, Inc., 1958.

Tokarczyk, Andrzej. *Trzydzieści Wyznań.* Warsaw: Wydawnictwo Książka i Wiedza, 1971.

Ware, Timothy. *The Orthodox Church.* Middlesex, England: Penguin Books, 1959.

Weiser, Francis X. *Handbook of Christian Feasts and Customs.* New York: Harcourt, Brace and Company, 1952.

Weston, Jessie L. *From Ritual to Romance.* New York: Doubleday, 1957.

The New Catholic Encyclopedia. Prepared by an editorial staff at the Catholic University of America, Washington, D.C. New York: McGraw-Hill Book Company, 1967.